EVERYMAN

and Its Dutch Original,
ELCKERLIJC

MIDDLE ENGLISH TEXTS SERIES

GENERAL EDITOR
Russell A. Peck
University of Rochester

ASSOCIATE EDITOR
Alan Lupack
University of Rochester

ASSISTANT EDITOR
Michael Livingston
University of Rochester

ADVISORY BOARD
Rita Copeland
University of Pennsylvania

Thomas G. Hahn
University of Rochester

Lisa Kiser
Ohio State University

R. A. Shoaf
University of Florida

Bonnie Wheeler
Southern Methodist University

The Middle English Texts Series is designed for classroom use. Its goal is to make available to teachers and students texts that occupy an important place in the literary and cultural canon but have not been readily available in student editions. The series does not include those authors, such as Chaucer, Langland, or Malory, whose English works are normally in print in good student editions. The focus is, instead, upon Middle English literature adjacent to those authors that teachers need in compiling the syllabuses they wish to teach. The editions maintain the linguistic integrity of the original work but within the parameters of modern reading conventions. The texts are printed in the modern alphabet and follow the practices of modern capitalization, word formation, and punctuation. Manuscript abbreviations are silently expanded, and *u/v* and *j/i* spellings are regularized according to modern orthography. Yogh (3) is transcribed as *g*, *gh*, *y*, or *s*, according to the sound in Modern English spelling to which it corresponds; thorn (þ) and eth (ð) are transcribed as *th*. Distinction between the second person pronoun and the definite article is made by spelling the one *thee* and the other *the*, and final -*e* that receives full syllabic value is accented (e.g., *charité*). Hard words, difficult phrases, and unusual idioms are glossed on the page, either in the right margin or at the foot of the page. Explanatory and textual notes appear at the end of the text, often along with a glossary. The editions include short introductions on the history of the work, its merits and points of topical interest, and brief working bibliographies.

EVERYMAN

and Its Dutch Original,
ELCKERLIJC

Edited by
Clifford Davidson,
Martin W. Walsh, and Ton J. Broos

Published for TEAMS
(The Consortium for the Teaching of the Middle Ages)
in Association with the University of Rochester

by

MEDIEVAL INSTITUTE PUBLICATIONS
Kalamazoo, Michigan
2007

Library of Congress Cataloging-in-Publication Data

Everyman.
  Everyman and its Dutch original, Elckerlijc / edited by Clifford Davidson, Martin W. Walsh, and Ton J. Broos.
    p. cm. -- (Middle English texts series)
  Includes bibliographical references.
  Parallel Middle English and Dutch texts; introduction and notes in English.
  ISBN-13: 978-1-58044-106-3 (pbk. : alk. paper)
  1. Christian ethics--Drama. 2. Moralities, English. 3. Moralities, Dutch. I. Davidson, Clifford. II. Walsh, Martin W. III. Broos, Ton J. IV. Elckerlijc. V. Title.
  PR1261.E8 2006
  822'.2--dc22

                                                          2006034489

ISBN 978-1-58044-106-3

CONTENTS

ACKNOWLEDGMENTS

For the Huth edition of *Everyman* our work was expedited by the Pollard and Redgrave series of microfilms and checked at the British Library. We are grateful for permission to use this edition of the play as well as the photograph of the title page. The selection from the 1493 edition of *The Golden Legend* was likewise facilitated by the Pollard and Redgrave series. For *Elckerlijc* we have been fortunate to be able to use the resources of the open source website of the Project Laurens Jz Coster, with the rather carelessly printed Vorsterman edition being emended as necessary by reference to the other early texts. Reference to the modern editions of both plays listed in our bibliography has also been most helpful in the preparation of the present volume, and in this we particularly mention those of *Everyman* prepared by W. W. Greg and A. C. Cawley and of *Elckerlijc* by Henri Logeman, Kornelis H. De Raaf, Bart Ramakers and Willem Wilmink, John Conley et al., and particularly H. J. E. Endepols and M. J. M. de Haan.

Permission to use the illustration of the booth stage was granted by *Comparative Drama* and W. M. H. Hummelen. We are also grateful to the Poculi Ludique Societas (PLS) for the photograph of the Toronto production of *Everyman*.

Fig. 1. Death, at left (Shelley Ledger), accosts Everyman (John Astington) in a Poculi Ludique Societas (PLS) production of *Everyman*, November–December 1979.

INTRODUCTION TO *EVERYMAN*

Everyman has been frequently anthologized and is generally represented as the best and most original example of the English morality play. The morality has popularly been claimed as a bridge between the medieval mysteries and secular Renaissance drama culminating in Shakespeare. While the excellence of *Everyman* is not in doubt, there are nevertheless several problems with the usual view.

1. *Everyman* is announced on the title page of the two complete editions printed by John Skot as "a treatyse . . . in maner of a morall playe," and this implies that it should be regarded as a literary or religious work rather than drama.[1] Further, there is no record of its production before the modern revival by William Poel in 1901. It could, of course, have been staged, though unrecorded, any number of times in the early sixteenth century, and would have been ideal for presentation as a school play. The fact that four printed editions are known (the two produced by the press of Richard Pynson are incomplete) argues for widespread popularity of the play in the decades prior to the time when Henry VIII's campaign of Protestantization began in earnest in 1536–39. Very possibly other editions, now lost, were originally printed. *Everyman* would have been quite consistent with the taste of the time for treatises on dying and on the spiritual life and hence would have served well as reading matter catering to the interests of the public both on the Continent and in early sixteenth-century English.[2]

2. The originality of *Everyman* is a matter to be set straight. The play certainly possesses originality in concept and execution, but not as entirely an English work. More than a century of scholarly discussion has in our view convincingly shown that *Everyman* is a translation and adaptation from the Dutch *Elckerlijc*, a work which is regarded in the Low Countries as an important part of Dutch literary heritage with notable productions being mounted well into the modern age, especially by Johan de Meester in 1907 and at the Holland Festival between 1950 and 1971.[3] It also stands behind Hugo von Hofmannsthal's *Jedermann: Das Spiel vom Sterben des reichen Mannes* of 1911. In earlier times *Elckerlijc* had even greater popularity as a readers' text, with translations and adaptations not only into English but also into Latin and German, even by the violently anti-Catholic Thomas Kirschmayer ("Naogeorgus"), whose *Mercator* dates from 1540. Adaptations known to have been staged include

---

[1] Comparison may be made with another work of ambiguous genre, *Of Gentylnes and Nobylité*, issued by the press of John Rastell in c. 1529 and written either by him or by John Heywood; the title page in this case provides the identification "compilid in maner of an enterlude" (Greg, *Bibliography*, nos. 8–9). For discussion, see Walker, *Politics of Performance*, pp. 16–17.

[2] See Bennett, *English Books and Readers*, pp. 65–76.

[3] For theater history, see Erenstein, ed., *Een theatergeschiedenis der Nederlanden*, pp. 555–57, 680–85.

Hans Sachs' *Ein Comedie von dem reichen sterbenden Menschen* of 1549 which derives from yet another version, *Hekastus* by Joris van Lankvelt (Macropedius), whose Latin text had been used for performance by his students at the Hieronymusschool in Utrecht in 1538.[4]

The influential 1536 Latin translation entitled *Homulus* by Christianus Ischyrius, rector of the Maastricht Latin School, provides the information that *Elckerlijc* won a prize at a theater contest in Brabant. Whether the prize was earned at the Antwerp *Landjuweel* (drama festival) of 1496 may be questioned, since the first known edition, issued by Christiaen Snellaert at Delft, has the same date, and there are differences that suggest a prior Dutch version. This even led the Dutch scholar R. Vos to assign the play to the early fifteenth century,[5] though of course a date closer to 1496 is more plausible. In any case, the play is definitely associated with city life since the story tells of the rich citizen who has forgotten how to receive salvation by sharing with the poor and showing his charity, and we know that Antwerp, for example, had an extensive tradition of Rhetoricians' plays that was flourishing prior to the sixteenth century.[6] These plays were presented on booth stages (fig. 1), temporary structures set up in the market square or similar location.[7]

In considering the matter of authorship, therefore, we thus need to look first to *Elckerlijc*, which, according to the translator of *Homulus*, was written by Petrus from Diest. Some have believed this to have been a reference to the Carthusian Petrus Dorlandus from the Zelem monastery near that town. Current opinion is that this author, who was a member of a strict and cloistered order[8] and who wrote mainly in Latin, is not a likely candidate for the creation of a play for the popular stage. The many secular and humorous details in the Dutch play are as significant as the theological knowledge is basic. There is no need to search for a scholarly theologian as author, though, in the light of the ending of the play, some connection with the late medieval mystical traditions of the Low Countries has been proposed.[9] The Flemish mystic Jan van Ruusbroek declared that in the heavenly virtue of charity we are above every

Fig. 2. Booth Stage. Joan Sadeler, after Marten de Vos, *De Redenrijcke Maeght Rhetorica*; Rijksprentenkabinet, Amsterdam.

[4] For the relation between the original Dutch play, early versions derived from it, and von Hofmansthal's *Jedermann*, see Adolf, "From *Everyman* and *Elckerlijc* to Hofmannsthal and Kafka."

[5] Vos, "De datering van de Elckerlijc."

[6] For a general survey of the Rhetoricians' plays, see Hummelen, "Drama of the Dutch Rhetoricians."

[7] See Hummelen, "Boundaries of the Rhetoricians' Stage."

[8] See Cross and Livingstone, eds., *Oxford Dictionary of the Christian Church, s.v.* "Carthusian Order."

[9] See Kazemier, "Elckerlijc."

human intellectual functioning, and his influence might be found in the idea that we deserve our place in Heaven according to our virtue.[10]

The specific Dutch text used by the anonymous translator who produced the English *Everyman* is not known and seems not to be extant, but probably was a printed edition such as Snellaert's edition of 1496 or the edition printed by Govaert Bac in Antwerp in c. 1501, both incomplete. A manuscript, now at the Bibliothèque Royale in Brussels (MS. IV 592), is based on a yet earlier text that is now lost. Unfortunately, this copy, written out by a certain P. Wilms in 1593–94, is a somewhat modernized text rather than an exact duplication of the fifteenth-century version on which it was based. The edition issued by Willem Vorsterman of Antwerp in c. 1525 — which bears close resemblance to the Bac edition — hence is traditionally used as the base for modern editions and is chosen in the present volume for the text to be included for comparison with *Everyman*.[11]

Though it is derived from the Dutch *Elckerlijc*, we still can say that *Everyman* is a superb work, though some scholars have faulted its translation of certain passages and its handling of some of the rhymes. We feel that it fully deserves its high reputation, but we also think that its origin in Continental theater deserves attention in the classroom, in anthologies, and in general theater studies, which unfortunately have generally been too little concerned with the niceties of scholarship. For this reason we have provided the original Dutch text, with translation, and the English *Everyman* on facing pages in the present edition.

3. Since *Everyman* is adapted from *Elckerlijc*, it is hard to see it as being a typical example of the English morality play. The early morality plays in English are few in number, and it is not possible to recognize in them a consistent theatrical tradition or, most importantly, a necessary step between the mystery cycles or religious biblical plays played in the main by amateurs and the professional drama of the great theatrical companies that were founded in the latter half of the sixteenth century. A very few plays — *The Pride of Life*, *The Castle of Perseverance*, *Mankind*, and *Wisdom* — hardly argue for anything other than an alternative theater mode (not a genre in itself) that sometimes occurred, mainly in East Anglian drama, before 1500. Remarkably, in contrast to the verifiable profusion of plays on saints' lives, there are no documents verifying performances of morality plays of this kind in England during this time,[12] though the plays named above surely were designed to be staged. Yet they are each very different from the other in numerous ways, including in the number of actors required for acting. Though needing a much smaller company of players than, say, *The Castle of Perseverance*, *Everyman*'s sixteen roles, even allowing for doubling, would have required more personnel than the "Foure men and a boy" specified for the play within-a-play offered by the Lord Cardinal's Players in *Sir Thomas More*[13] and given by David Bevington as more or less a pre-1576 norm for a traveling company.[14] The nature of the early morality in England indeed remains obscure, and a very likely theory is that some plays in this

---

[10] Ibid., pp. 123–24.

[11] The text of the three editions and the manuscript have been printed in a diplomatic edition by de Haan, *De Spiegel der Zaligheid van Elckerlijc*. The Vorsterman text has most recently been edited and translated into modern Dutch by Ramakers and Wilmink, *Mariken van Nieumeghen & Elckerlijc*.

[12] See Wasson, "Morality Play." For the extensive dramatic traditions involving saints, see the list compiled by Davidson, "Saint Plays and Pageants of Medieval Britain."

[13] *Sir Thomas More* 4.1.54 (*Shakespeare Apocrypha*, ed. Brooke, p. 403).

[14] See Bevington, *From* Mankind *to* Marlowe, pp. 68–85.

mode were used as mayors' plays to be presented before the mayor without remuneration to show that the troupe is handling religious themes legitimately. Such a mayor's play, albeit at a much later date, in the 1570s, at Gloucester, was described by R. Willis. This was *The Cradle of Security*, which like *Everyman* could be construed as a warning of the coming Judgment predicted by the Bible when everyone, from high to low in the society, would be called to account.[15] But with the lack of evidence concerning moralities prior to the Reformation in England we cannot be sure that there ever was a recognizable genre until the sixteenth century. For the theatrical tradition into which *Everyman* must be placed we therefore need to look to the Continental evidence.

Like *The Cradle of Security*, which Willis as an old man of seventy-five was able to recall vividly from his childhood in his *Mount Tabor* (1639), *Everyman* and the Dutch *Elckerlijc* are allegorical plays. About allegorical drama over the years there have been some serious misconceptions such as evidenced in a statement by an anonymous early nineteenth-century writer in the *Retrospective Review*, who complained about the lack of plot, character, and "scenic illusion" and wondered how such plays "should have attracted such attention and excited such interest amongst all ranks of society."[16] Hence it may come as a surprise that such a form could so impress a person that as an aging adult Willis found the play "as fresh in my memory, as if I had seen it newly acted."[17] The current understanding of allegory still often remains too much under the spell of critics such as Coleridge, who defined it as "but a translation of abstract notions into a picture-language, which is itself but an abstraction from objects of the senses; the principal being more worthless even than its phantom proxy, both alike unsubstantial, and the former shapeless to boot."[18] Coleridge was merely affirming Enlightenment prejudices which, applied to the morality drama, would be implied in John Payne Collier's assessment: "A Moral, or Moral-play, is a drama, the characters of which are allegorical, abstract, or symbolical, and the story of which is intended to convey a lesson for the better conduct of human life."[19] But in actuality, as students of Dante's *Commedia* have long known, this view of allegory assumes a modern mechanistic world in which external things no longer mask psychological and spiritual realities.[20] Further, as the researches of Natalie Crohn Schmitt and Robert Potter indicate, when allegorical figures such as Everyman, Good Deeds, and Knowledge are presented by actors — or, in the case of *Every-*

---

[15] Douglas and Greenfield, eds., *Records of Early English Drama: Cumberland, Westmorland, Gloucestershire*, pp. 362–64. The text of *The Cradle of Security* is lost, but that it was well known is suggested by the inclusion of the title among the plays offered for acting by the Lord Cardinal's Players in *Sir Thomas More* 4.1.41–42 (*Shakespeare Apocrypha*, ed. Brooke, p. 403).

[16] "Mysteries, Moralities, and Other Early Dramas," *Retrospective Review* 1 (1820): 332–35, as quoted by Potter, *English Morality Play*, p. 212.

[17] Douglas and Greenfield, eds., *Records of Early English Drama: Cumberland, Westmorland, Gloucestershire*, p. 363.

[18] Coleridge, *Statesman's Manual*, in *Complete Works*, ed. Shedd, 1:437–38.

[19] Collier, *History of English Dramatic Poetry*, 2:287n. Less hostile, but nevertheless still under the influence of this view, was Mackenzie, whose definition of the genre has been much quoted: "A morality is a play, allegorical in nature, which has for its main object the teaching of some lesson for the guidance of life, and in which the principal characters are personified abstractions or highly universalized types" (*English Moralities from the Point of View of Allegory*, p. 9).

[20] See, for example, Piehler, *Visionary Landscape*, p. 11 and *passim*.

man, are possibly *imagined* to be presented by actual persons — these characters take on a life of their own that can be very powerful.[21] They may be rooted in ideas, but they are given a larger identity and humanized when they are joined with living actors and given visible presence on stage.

In the early sixteenth century — a time when mortality was always an immediate threat and hence when there was intense concern with death and its aftermath — the power of such a play as *Everyman*, even if read rather than staged, would presumably have been more deeply felt than today and would have left a more powerful lasting impression. The intended visual effect, whether on stage or in the imaginations of readers, was to create a kind of memory theater to which the mind would return again and again as a way of being reminded in symbolic terms of human mortality and the consequences of one's actions in this life.[22] It will need to be remembered that the mortality rate, especially in urban areas, was often greater than the birth rate,[23] and in cities an influx of people from outside the walls was needed to maintain the population level. In the late fifteenth and early sixteenth centuries, important cities such as Coventry and Norwich were in a state of crisis on account of the severe decline in their populations.[24] Readers of *Everyman* and its potential audience as a stage play would have had an awareness of these larger demographic factors. The character Everyman is a relatively young male, but the high mortality rate for men as well as women simply had to be a cause of severe anxiety. Death was a destabilizer of family and the community alike in addition to being the source of personal fear, which during this period led either to denial or to recognition of its implications for life beyond the grave. This period in history has been identified as an age of bacteria,[25] and of course there was no social democratic safety net. In 1490 William Caxton had published *A Lityll Treatise Spekynge of the Art and Crafte to Knowe Well to Dye*, followed by other editions and versions of the same work. A. C. Cawley especially notes its relevance for *Everyman* since in one of the sections on the temptations which the dying man faces it identifies too much attention to "outwarde thinges," including family, friends, and riches.[26] Life's terminus is examined here, and advice is given about how to meet death and to prepare for the life hereafter.

A discussion of this motif should perhaps not neglect reference to the painting *The Death of a Miser* by Hieronymus Bosch in the National Gallery of Art, Washington, D.C.[27] This work, from c. 1490 and hence roughly contemporary with the writing of *Elckerlijc*, may be

---

[21] Schmitt, "Idea of a Person"; Potter, *English Morality Play*, p. 34 and *passim*.

[22] From antiquity memory was commonly compared to a wax tablet in which images could make an impression and take hold in the mind; see Carruthers, *Book of Memory*, pp. 27–30.

[23] See Slack, "Mortality Crises and Epidemic Disease."

[24] See Phythian-Adams, *Desolation of a City*.

[25] See Gottfried, *Epidemic Disease*.

[26] *Everyman*, ed. Cawley, pp. xvi–xvii; see also Spinrad, "Last Temptation of Everyman," especially pp. 187–88, and, for a review of the context, Beaty, *Craft of Dying*, pp. 1–48, as well as the review of iconography in Mâle, *Religious Art in France*, pp. 348–55, and the listing by the editor of this English edition (on p. 529n116) of more recent studies not originally available to Mâle. For the Dutch *ars moriendi* tradition, see de Geus et al., eds., *Een scone Leeringe om salich te sterven*. A case can be made for the specific influence on *Everyman* of the textual and visual representation of the stages of dying in *The Arte and Crafte to Knowe Well to Dye*; see the summary in Beaty, *Craft of Dying*, p. 34.

[27] Gibson, *Hieronymus Bosch*, figs. 31–32.

seen as an important analogue to the drama and its English adaptation. To be sure, there are differences, for the rich man in the painting is old rather than young, and, it would appear from the details that are shown, he is unlikely to achieve salvation. As Walter S. Gibson explains, "his guardian angel supports him and attempts to draw his attention to the crucifix in the window above, but he cannot draw his mind from the earthly possessions he must leave behind; one hand reaches out almost automatically to clutch the bag of gold offered by a demon."[28] A chest open at the foot of the bed shows a man, presumably the miser prior to his terminal illness, dropping a coin into an open bag that is being held up by a demon. At the left the figure of Death is making his appearance at a door; he has a dart in his hand that is aimed directly at the dying man in the bed. The tension between the love of goods and the necessity of a good death as described by the treatises on the art of dying is graphically depicted here as it is in *Everyman* and its Dutch source.

4. In *Everyman*, as had been the case in *Elckerlijc*, the art of dying was indeed to be virtually the substance of the play. The effect that is achieved, however, is timeless and may be compared with the presentation of Death in Ingmar Bergman's 1956 screenplay *The Seventh Seal*, set in the time of the Black Death but reflecting modern fears of a nuclear apocalypse.[29] In *Everyman* there is a strong emphasis on the shock of recognition when Death comes to the protagonist and announces to him that he must die. This is of course exactly what happens in the Dance of Death,[30] for which John Lydgate provided translations of the French text that accompanied the paintings in the Cemetery of the Innocents at Paris. These would be widely known and imitated, for Lydgate's verses and copies of the paintings at Paris were given great visibility on account of being prominently displayed in the cloisters of St. Paul's Cathedral in London. In Sir William Dugdale's description, the portrayal was of "the picture of Death leading away all estates."[31] The Dance of Death derived from the concern with death that developed after the arrival of the Black Death in 1348–49. In Lydgate's text and in the illustrations representing the arrest of human beings by the sinister figure that represented mortality, Death comes as if with extreme suddenness to each individual, from the highest (pope, emperor) to the lowest (child, clerk, hermit). So it is in the single scene that remains at St. Andrew's Church in Norwich, where a bishop in full episcopal vestments is being taken by the right hand by a cadaverous figure draped with a shroud. The bishop, who is turning away from the unwished visitor, is standing on a tile floor reminiscent of a chessboard and hence indicative of the role of fortune or chance in bringing about one's end.[32] Lydgate's text, in the Lansdowne manuscript, gives this victim the following response:

> Of these tidynges I am no thyng glaad
> Which Deth to me so sodeynly doth bryng;
> It makith my face and countenaunce ful saad. . . .[33]

---

[28] Ibid., p. 46.

[29] For the filmscript (in translation), see Bergman, *Four Screen Plays*, pp. 95–164.

[30] An example in which Death appears to a fashionably dressed young man like Everyman is to be seen in a panel painting at Newark-on-Trent (Tasker, *Encyclopedia of Medieval Church Art*, p. 184, fig. 6.22). See also Clark, *Dance of Death*, pp. 9–10.

[31] Dugdale, *History of St. Pauls Cathedral in London*, pp. 131–32.

[32] See King, "Pre-Reformation Painted Glass in St. Andrew's Church, Norwich."

[33] Lydgate, *Dance of Death*, ed. Warren, p. 25.

In words which seem to refer directly to the action of *Everyman*, the translator in the Ellesmere manuscript announces that the dance at St. Innocents in Paris — and, consequently, in English versions — "Portreied is with al the surplusage / To shewe this worlde is but a pilgrimage."[34]

At Stratford-upon-Avon, Dance of Death paintings and verses on the north wall of the nave of the Guild Chapel that would for some time survive the Elizabethan desecration of religious images — and remain visible into the lifetime of William Shakespeare — are now very fragmentary but in that state hidden under paneling that was put in place in the 1950s.[35] The king's dying words in this wall painting, as recorded by Wilfrid Puddephat, are: "we shall all to dede ashes tourne."[36]

The connection between this iconography and *Everyman* is made even more explicit in the woodcuts that appear on the title pages of the Huth and Huntington Library editions of the play printed by John Skot (fig. 2). In each case two separate woodcuts are brought together to show the figure of Everyman at the left and on the right a cadaverous Death in a graveyard who is holding a tomb cover and pointing generally in the direction of his victim. These woodcuts in no sense are related to any production of the play, either real or theoretical. The Everyman figure is printed from a factotum block that had originated with the Parisian printer Antoine Vérard, while Death is a copy of a woodcut that had been used in a book printed earlier by Wynkyn de Worde, in turn a copy from Vérard's *Kalendrier et compost des bergiers* (1493).[37] Together they do make an allusion to the Dance of Death that could not at that time have been missed.[38]

Faced with death's certainty — and the uncertainty of the time of its coming, particularly in a historical period of widespread plague and other afflictions — as well as the inevitability of the hereafter, what is one to do? *Everyman* speaks to this dilemma, even to those who would be indifferent to the existential realities that were generally assumed by the people of the time. The play's advice does not extend, however, to the encouragement of a detached mystical piety or monastic retreat from the world. It is very far from the separation from society that was found among the highly respected Carthusians, among whom Sir Thomas More spent four years "in devotion and prayer" while considering what direction his life should take.[39] Rather, in presenting a figure who has been very much in the world — indeed, a world of fashionable clothes and style of living — the play reflects an affluent

---

[34] Ibid., p. 4.

[35] Puddephat, "Mural Paintings of the Dance of Death"; Davidson, *Guild Chapel Wall Paintings*, pp. 6–9, 50–55, pls. 19–20.

[36] Quoted from Stratford-upon-Avon, Birthplace Trust Records office, DR399/5/5, in Davidson, *Guild Chapel Wall Paintings*, p. 52.

[37] See Davidson, *Illustrations of the Stage*, pp. 132–35, and, for Vérard's woodcut, see for convenience Briesemeister, *Bilder des Todes*, fig. 126. The reverse title page of the Huth edition has woodcuts, including the Everyman figure from the title page, along with others purporting to illustrate Fellowship, Beauty, Discretion, Strength, and Kindred; see Davidson, *Illustrations of the Stage*, fig. 157.

[38] The woodcuts in the Skot editions of *Everyman* echo the woodcut on the title page of the Vorsterman edition of *Elckerlijc*. This illustration shows Death with a spear about to stab a young man who has thrown up his hands in terror; see *Elckerlijc*, ed. Logeman, p. 100. The scene is not set in a cemetery, and is a rather crude representation, though at least it is printed from a single block. See also our note to *Everyman*, line 76, below.

[39] Roper, *Lyfe of Sir Thomas Moore, Knighte*, ed. Hitchcock, p. 6.

and secure position in the society. It is, in fact, consistent with the kind of society in which the Dutch Rhetoricians' plays such as *Elckerlijc* were written and produced. As such, it was a play world that was easily adaptable to the English scene, whether aristocratic or mercantile. The protagonist is one who, because he has laid up treasures on earth, has been in a position to do good deeds, but he has been very lax about it and instead has pursued enjoyment and wealth, the latter hoarded instead of being shared with the poor and needy. By so doing, he has not been able to lengthen his life, nor has he gained a secure place in the afterlife. Now he must, as the medieval mystics knew, endure the solitariness of leaving behind all that has given him comfort in this world.[40]

The parable of the talents in Matthew 25:14–30, to which V. A. Kolve has called attention in an influential article, will provide a measure of how Everyman has fallen short in his care for the talent (in the modern signification of the term) and the wealth that has been entrusted to him.[41] In commercial terms, his accounts are not in order or ready for the audit before the divine Judge. Everyman is thus unprepared for the final "rekenynge" that will be demanded of him.[42] For this reason he is in danger of being "cast into outer darkness" where there "shall be weeping and gnashing of teeth." But the other parables in Matthew 25 are also relevant. Everyman at the beginning of the play is ominously like the foolish virgins who fail to keep their lamps burning for the moment when the Bridegroom comes without warning, for he indeed has failed to keep in mind the uncertainty of life and the certainty of having to be ready for the arrival of the one who will either take him into the marriage feast or have him denied entrance. But the ethic promoted by the play is even more directly influenced by the concluding parable of the chapter (Matthew 25:33–46) which describes the coming down of the Son of Man with his angels to sit upon "the throne of glory." Here the acceptance or rejection of those who have been gathered from all time and all nations will be dependent upon whether the individuals seeking to enter bliss have performed the Corporal Acts of Mercy: feeding the hungry, giving drink to the thirsty, providing shelter for the homeless and the stranger, clothing the naked, caring for the sick, and visiting prisoners — to which was added the burial of the dead. In *Everyman* we are reminded of these acts whenever "saint charyté" — that is, "holy charity" — is invoked. Such charitable deeds, rather than cheating, stealing, or looting the public in order to create and hold personal wealth, have permanent viability. Those who will not have done them will be cursed and thrown into the "everlasting fire, which was prepared for the devil and his angels."

However, according to Catholic theology there is hope even for the stingy capitalist if he undergoes penance, beginning with confession to a priest, whose absolution provides a conditional forgiveness of sins — conditional on the subject's contrition and sincere willingness

---

[40] See Riehle, *Middle English Mystics*, p. 17.

[41] Kolve, "*Everyman* and the Parable of the Talents."

[42] The expression "Day of Reckoning" in some form seems to have been used very early for the day of the Last Judgment, and this is what is implied in *Everyman*. "Rekenynge" (Dutch: "rekeninghe") in the context of the play in *Elckerlijc* indicates calculating the value of one's good deeds, as these necessarily derive from virtue, toward salvation or of one's debits toward damnation in the context of the *psychostasis* or weighing of souls. John Audelay understood such good deeds to involve having "peté of the pore" — deeds that are required if one should wish not to "be schamyd and chent / When thou art callid to thi rekynyng; / Ther God and mon schal be present, / And al the world on fuyre brenyng / The[e] to afray" (*Poems*, ed. Whiting, p. 9).

to carry through the final stage of satisfaction, including making amends, that will result in the perfect cleansing of the soul. In Everyman's case, he must make restitution for the wrongs he has done, and he must share the remainder of his wealth with those in need. In other words, he must not do what the miser would do: he must not deny assistance to the needy, for he must act according to the moral standards established in the Corporal Acts of Mercy. His only recourse is to make the necessary provisions in his will before he proceeds to the final moment of his life and that terrifying instant when he must look into the grave which is to receive him.

5. *Everyman*, like *Elckerlijc*, is thus not a straightforward sermon about the necessity for reformation of one's life but rather is designed to present an existential experience of imaginative participation in facing the inevitable. Its method is, if we may use the terminology developed by the theologian Robert C. Neville, "symbolic engagement," in which the reader or audience is brought into a symbolic action in a way more immediate than by reading an abstract presentation concerning death. Though never esoteric, the theological underpinning, as the notes to the present edition will demonstrate, is throughout a presence in the play. Yet the play's intent is not to teach abstract doctrine but to move its readership or audience emotionally and intellectually toward a resolution that emphasizes both one's individual responsibility and the importance of being connected in this life with one's community. *Everyman* differs from the confrontation with death in a modern sensational terror film such as *The Night of the Living Dead*, which is designed to titillate rather than to engage deeply or to cause one to think of life's realities.

One source for the story dramatized in *Elckerlijc* and subsequently in *Everyman* is a Buddhist parable of false friends that very early migrated to the West (see Appendix).[43] The version that the author of the Dutch play most likely knew was the one included in the story of Barlaam and Josaphat in the popular *Golden Legend* of Jacobus de Voragine, which also was very well known in England. Here three friends, two of whom represent aspects of worldly pleasure and vanity, are sought out by a man who, having fallen into mortal peril, has been summoned to the king.[44] He requests assistance from the first (riches), whom he loved even more than himself, but he is only offered two gowns, interpreted as garments for his burial.[45] The man then goes to the second (kinsmen), whom he loved as much as himself. He also refuses. In desperation, the man goes to the third friend, whom he has not loved very much at all. This friend, however, responds quite differently and grants him the help that he needs. He represents good deeds, faith, hope, and charity, and will go ahead of the man to intercede for him with the king. A similar version is contained in the extended story of Barlaam and Josaphat contained in Cambridge University Library, Peterhouse MS 257,

---

[43] The story of the false friends in the play requires, however, to be understood in the context described by Conley, "Doctrine of Friendship in *Everyman*." For the earliest known stage of the parable, see the Georgian version, believed to be derived ultimately from the Sanskrit tradition by way of lost Manichaean and Arabic texts, as translated by Lang, *Wisdom of Balahvar*, pp. 82–83. For a listing of some other Western versions of the parable, see *Barlam and Iosaphat*, ed. Hirsch, p. 201.

[44] See, for example, British Library MS Egerton 876, fol. 303v, as transcribed by Keiko Ikegami (*Barlaam and Josaphat*, p.166), and, for Caxton's translation of the parable in *The Golden Legend*, the Appendix to the present volume.

[45] This interpretation of the gowns is present in the Georgian version of the parable (*Wisdom of Balahvar*, pp. 65, 82–83). That the translator of *Everyman* was vaguely familiar with this point is suggested by lines 292–93, but he gets things turned around since he has Fellowship say to the protagonist, "Nay, and thou wolde gyve me a new gowne, / I wyll not one fote with thee goo."

where the transgression of the protagonist is a "dette of ten thousande besauntys that he aught the kynge" while the friends are riches, kindred, and "mannys good workys. That is, feith, hope, charite, almasdede, and al other vertuys whych gone before us ere we deye and prayen God for us, that he wyl delyvere us fro oure crewel enmyes that maken grete accusacions agens us, and ever awayten to take us and to distroye."[46]

Variant versions of the parable also appear in the *Gesta Romanorum*[47] and in other sources. In a sermon in British Library MS Royal 18.B.xxiii, four friends are asked for assistance when the protagonist of the story has "trespased agenys the kynge of the londe, and so had forfette agenys the lawe that he was [w]urthye to die." The first (the world) refuses and says that he will do no more than provide a burial cloth. The second (kindred) also refuses to help a felon beyond coming with him to his execution, while the third (the devil) offers to "helpe to hange hym," for he too is "a frend to a tyme, but he dwelleth not in the daye of tribulacion." But the fourth friend (Christ), for whom he had least liking, agrees to go with him to ask forgiveness of the king and even offers to die in his stead.[48] Here too the order of the false friends does not precisely match those in the play, and it may be that the adaptation of the parable initially for the Flemish stage could have been based on a text that, though unknown to us, might have provided more details for the playwright to draw upon. To be sure, structurally the Dutch and English plays are more complex than this parable in any of its forms — or, for that matter, in any version likely to have existed — with a carefully constructed plot that is built on the motif of a "double desertion" pattern in which totally false friends first leave him, as do friends who logically cannot help him across into the life beyond this life though they have been useful at stages along the way.[49] An exemplum detailing the desertion of strength, beauty, and worldly wisdom as well as earthly goods from the dying man contained in a sermon by the Dominican John Bromyard is reported by G. R. Owst, but here the sinner is destined for Hell fire rather than the Heaven to which Everyman will aspire following his confession.[50] It is, after all, the second set of desertions at the conclusion of the drama that is most moving, since this signals the very end of one's life with a finality that is terrifying.[51]

6. *Everyman*, as noted above, is represented by four separate printings, two of which are incomplete (the Bodleian copy is actually a fragment only), between c. 1510 and c. 1529. The copy chosen as the basis for the present text was printed by John Skot and is found in the Huth collection (Huth 32) housed at the British Library. This printing, dated c. 1530–35, was declared by W. W. Greg to be the edition that is possibly closest to the original English text prepared by the translator,[52] and may be compared with the copy, sometimes called the

---

[46] *Barlam and Iosaphat*, ed. Hirsh, pp. 57–59.

[47] See *Early English Versions of the Gesta Romanorum*, ed. Herrtage, pp. 127–32.

[48] *Middle English Sermons*, ed. Ross, pp. 86–89.

[49] See Johnson, "Double Desertion."

[50] Owst, *Literature and Pulpit in Medieval England*, pp. 527–28, citing John Bromyard, *Summa Predicantium, s.v.* "Mors"; attention is called to this passage by Johnson, "Double Desertion," p. 86.

[51] The anxiety expressed in the second set of desertions brings into question the analysis of Van Laan, "*Everyman*: A Structural Analysis," who attempts to see a conventional pattern of rising and falling action in a play that we believe defies simplistic formal analysis.

[52] Greg, *Bibliography of the English Printed Drama* 1.4.

Britwell copy, which was also printed by Skot, in the Huntington Library, and with the incomplete British Library copy printed by Pynson and the Pynson fragment in the Bodleian Library. We have corrected the Huth text when warranted with readings from the other editions, and significant differences between them are cited in the textual notes. Speech headings have been regularized, as have the letters *u/v* and *i/j*. Abbreviations have been spelled out. It should be mentioned that biblical citations in our critical notes are to the Douay-Rheims translation.

The text of *Elckerlijc* in this volume, presented for the purpose of comparison with *Everyman*, follows the edition published by Vorsterman, whose reputation as a printer was, it should be noted, not stellar since the books produced by him were marred by compositors' mistakes and other errors. We have corrected minor errors mainly by reference to the other early editions and the late manuscript copy (adding, for instance, a line from the Brussels manuscript at line 62). Because the emphasis of the present edition is on *Everyman*, we have not found it necessary to include a separate set of notes to *Elckerlijc*. Readers with a reading knowledge of the Dutch language are directed to the modern editions of the play listed in our bibliography since they contain valuable critical and textual notes. In particular, we would refer readers to the edition of A. van Elslander (1985), which can be found online.[53] Elslander's edition provides variants from all versions in addition to his own edited text and introduction. Although Elslander's base text is not Huth, we have worked to corroborate our line numbers with his in order to facilitate cross-referencing between the editions. The translation that accompanies our Dutch text is intended to be a fairly literal English version for comparison with the Middle English *Everyman* for non-Dutch readers.

THE STAGE HISTORY OF *EVERYMAN*

As noted above, the first performance of *Everyman* of which we have record was in July 1901 when it was given three Saturday productions by William Poel in an outdoor staging at the Charterhouse in London. The figure of Death in this production was given a trumpet and drum, but not the dart, a sign of his lethal nature,[54] as a sign of his arrival to announce to Everyman his imminent mortality. As a symbolic representation the trumpet is not out of line with traditional iconography.[55] On the whole, Poel's production may be described as pre-Raphaelite, in part because the costumes, borrowed from Holman Hunt, were copies of designs in Flemish tapestries.

Medieval drama at this time was still regarded with suspicion, and, as Poel's biographer reports, his request to present the play in the Westminster Abbey cloisters had been refused.[56]

---

[53] http://www.dbnl.org/tekst/_elc001elck01/

[54] Death also kills a mankind figure with a spear in Thomas Chaundler's Latin morality, *Liber Apologeticus de Omni Statu Humanae Naturae*, ed. Shoukri, pl. 13; see also Davidson, *Illustrations of the Stage and Acting*, p. 64, fig. 66. So too Death wields a dart or "launce," similarly struck into Mankind's "herte rote," in *The Castle of Perseverance* (lines 2807, 2842). Death's dart, like the scythe which signifies his role as the grim reaper, frequently appears in iconography; see, for example, Briesemeister, *Bilder des Todes*, passim. But, as noted above, the woodcut on the title page of the Vorsterman edition of *Elkerlijc* holds a spear with which he is about to kill the protagonist.

[55] See Briesemeister, *Bilder des Todes*, figs. 1, 3, 32, 34, and 38.

[56] Speaight, *William Poel*, p. 161.

Some aspects of this initial production, including the casting of a woman as Everyman, may be looked on as oddities, but it was nevertheless a spectacular success, though the depiction of Adonai (played by Poel himself) as an old man with gray beard[57] continued to scandalize some and to transgress against the prohibition in English law against depicting God on stage as blasphemous.[58] When the play, under a new director, Ben Greet, was moved to New York for the 1902–03 season, the furor was louder in spite of moving God offstage, but this production, which was the first performance in America on an approximation of a Renaissance stage, also would subsequently be very successful and would tour as far west as St. Louis.[59]

Poel had come to the play during a period of grief after the death of his mother. As a drama incorporating a universal theme, *Everyman* appealed to him in spite of its theology, with which he had little sympathy.[60] It was, however, in Greet's American stagings that the play suffered drastically from the pruning away of the didactic and more overtly theological matter contained in the text.[61] In England, Poel subsequently turned *Everyman* over to Nugent Monck, whose Maddermarket Players would bring the play in 1929 to the Canterbury Festival,[62] later the venue for T. S. Eliot's *Murder in the Cathedral* (1935) and Charles Williams' *Cranmer* (1936).[63]

The play seems to have suffered much more from directors of some later productions, most egregiously in a television version presented on Omnibus, a series funded by the Ford Foundation, on 5 April 1953. A review by Erling Larsen which found its way into a little magazine of the time complained that the mystery permeating the original play "lasted perhaps fifteen seconds," then shifted into "pure soap-opera with the play rewritten so that hardly a line was recognizable and the idea behind the play *in toto* altered."[64] But even in a production of the play at the Guthrie Theatre in Minneapolis during the 1974–75 season very odd things happened as the role of Everyman was distributed to each of the actors in turn, while for a finale the members of the cast walked through the audience inappropriately singing "Bless This House" by May H. Brahe. In the Steppenwolf Theatre Company performances of 1994–95 in Chicago, the choice of the person to take on the role Everyman was made by chance at the beginning of the play as books were passed out to each of four actors; the one who received the book with the protagonist's part would then be Everyman. According to Robert Potter's

---

[57] Ibid., pl. facing p. 224.

[58] See Elliott, *Playing God*, pp. 17–18, 42–44, for commentary on the law and its loopholes as exploited by Poel, the changes which satisfied the censor in commercial theaters, and the official denial in one instance that God had ever been presented on stage.

[59] Potter, *English Morality Play*, pp. 222–25; Cole, "Elizabethan Stages and Open-Air Stages."

[60] Poel later denounced the theology of the play and indicated that he was "moving away" from the drama in an interview; see Speaight, *William Poel*, p. 166.

[61] Potter, *English Morality Play*, p. 225.

[62] Pickering, *Drama in the Cathedral*, pp. 48–50.

[63] Charles Williams' *Cranmer*, which dramatized the accomplishments and martyrdom of the reforming archbishop of Canterbury Thomas Cranmer, is of particular interest here on account of the playwright's use of a skeletal Death-like character that must have been influenced by *Everyman*; see Browne and Browne, *Two in One*, pp. 102–07.

[64] Larsen, "All Things to Everyman." Some further productions and adaptations of interest, including a puppet production by Peter Arnott, are noted by Schreiber, "*Everyman* in America."

report on the production, Death was an alluring woman who "embraces Everyman literally as well as figuratively, in delivering her message."[65] In this the director, Frank Galati, was departing from the iconography of Death coming as a shock and instead showing how mortality can come about as the ultimate result of very tempting behavior. The terror represented by Death's arrival in this case was, however, perhaps not diminished.

The Los Angeles-based Cornerstone Theatre Company produced its *Everyman in the Mall* in 1994 at the Santa Monica Place Mall, a production revived in 1997–98. In this case the medieval text was used to assault contemporary American consumerism. The audience was taken on a pilgrimage from narrow service corridors into the glittering arcade of the mall itself where real shops (e.g., a jewelry store) were used as backdrops. The production successfully blended the authentic text and modern interpolations and was energized by a transformational acting style with multiple Deaths, Everymans male and female, and so forth. Kindred and Cousin, two clowns, were never able to get off a down escalator to aid Everyman. Goods was a seductive mannikin; Knowledge, Confession, and Penance were minority custodial staff. The production ended with a harrowingly real cardiac arrest that brought the naked truth of Death into the fantasy world of American materialism.[66]

Another professional production of *Everyman* was introduced by the Royal Shakespeare Company at Stratford-upon-Avon in 1996. Though some changes were made in the roles (for example, Five Wits was also Discretion), all the play's lines were spoken, albeit along with stage action very different from what a sixteenth-century audience would have expected or accepted. Death again was a woman who came to dance with Everyman, hence giving motivation to his/her first words: "Everyman, stonde styll." When other characters entered as a circus troupe, the reviewer Marion O'Connor at first mistook them for Hell's Angels. O'Connor nevertheless found the production, which emphasized the relationships between the characters and also the importance of the visual dimension of the play, to be a "compelling" performance and "wholly appropriate to the ideology of the play."[67]

Some of the most successful and the most innovative productions of *Everyman* have been those mounted by university troupes. The University of Toronto's PLS (Poculi Ludique Societas) had the advantage of a performance text prepared by John Astington with extensive director's notes on acting (fig. 1).[68] A performance at St. Martin's College, Olympia, Washington, in 1992 chose to take the journey of life iconography literally as the structuring device for a processional production that led through the campus and used the scene to full advantage in placing Everyman within a familiar contemporary setting. Its conclusion was actually in a graveyard, the location where Everyman is confronted with Death in the woodcuts on the title page of the Huth and Huntington editions printed by John Skot.[69] Another university production, by the Workshop Theatre of the University of Leeds in 1997, was praised by James Cummings for not "being forced to convey messages that were not

[65] "Census of Medieval Drama Productions," 192–93.

[66] Robert Potter, "*Everyman* at the Millennium," unpublished paper read at the international colloquium of the Société Internationale pour l'etude du Théâtre Médiéval at Groningen, The Netherlands, in 2001.

[67] O'Connor, "*Everyman, The Creation* and *The Passion*."

[68] *Everyman*, ed. Astington.

[69] Greenfield, "Processional *Everyman* at St. Martin's College."

originally intended"; thus the "strength of the actors' skill" was allowed to "bring across the original meanings with clarity and effectiveness."[70]

EARLY EDITIONS OF *EVERYMAN*

Indexed as items 10603–06 in Pollard and Redgrave, eds., *Short-Title Catalogue*:

- [*Everyman*.] London: Richard Pynson, [c. 1510–25]. British Library C.21.c.17 (*STC* 10603).
- [*Everyman*.] London: Richard Pynson, [c. 1525–30]. Douce Fragment, Bodleian Library (*STC* 10604).
- *The Somonyng of Everyman*. London: John Skot, [c. 1525–30]. British Library, Huth 32 (*STC* 10605). [Base Text.]
- *The Somonynge of Everyman*. London: John Skot, [c. 1530–35]. Huntington Library, formerly at Britwell Court (*STC* 10606).

Everyman has been frequently printed, and hence those editions cited in the bibliography are only the most important editions as well as the major recent anthologies that contain the play.

MANUSCRIPT AND EARLY EDITIONS OF *ELCKERLIJC*

- *Den Spiegel der Salicheyt*. Brussels, Bibliothèque Royale MS. IV–592.

- *Elckerlijck*. Delft: Snellaert, 1496.
- *Den Spyeghel der Salicheyt van Elckerlyc*. Antwerp: William Vorsterman, [c. 1496]. [Base text.]
- *Den Spiegel der Salicheit van Elckerlijc*. Antwerp: Govaert Bac, [c. 1501].

---

[70] "Census of Medieval Drama Productions," 128.

EVERYMAN

and Its Dutch Original,
ELCKERLIJC

Fig. 3. Title Page of *Everyman*. British Library, Huth 32. By permission of the British Library.

DEN SPYEGHEL DER SALICHEYT VAN ELCKERLIJC

Hoe dat elckerlijc mensche wert ghedaecht Gode rekeninghe te doen.

Hier beghint een schoon boecxken, ghemaect in den maniere van eenen speele ofte esbatemente op elckerlijc mensche.

. . .

Ende inden eersten spreekt God Almachtich aldus:

GOD   Ick sie boven uut mijnen throne
        Dat al dat is int smenschen persone
        Leeft uut vresen, onbekent.
        Oec sie ic tvolc also verblent
5   In sonden, si en kennen mi niet voer God.

[Translation of Dutch *Elckerlijc*]

THE MIRROR OF EVERYMAN'S SALVATION

How Everyman is summoned to give a reckoning to God.

Here begins a nice little book made in the manner of a play or drama on every human being.

. . .

THE SOMONYNG OF EVERYMAN

Here begynneth a treatyse how the hye Fader of Heven sendeth Dethe to somon every creature to come and gyve a counte of theyr lyves in this worlde, and is in maner of a morall playe.

MESSENGER	I pray you all gyve your audyence	
	And here this matter with reverence,	*hear*
	By fygure a morall playe.	*In form; morality*
	The Somonyng of Everyman called it is	*Summoning*
5	That of our lyves and endynge shewes	*shows*
	How transytory we be all daye.	*always*
	This matter is wonderous precyous,	
	But the intente of it is more gracyous	
	And swete to bere awaye.	
10	This story sayeth: man in the begynnynge,	
	Loke well and take good hede to the endynge,	
	Be you never so gaye.	
	Ye thynke synne in the begynnynge full swete	
	Whiche in the ende causeth thy soule to wepe	
15	Whan the body lyeth in claye.	
	Here shall you se how Felawshyp and Jolyté	*Joy*
	Bothe, Strengthe, Pleasure, and Beauté,	
	Wyll vade from thee as floure in Maye,	*fade; flower*
	For ye shall here how our Heven Kenge	*hear; Heaven's King*
20	Calleth Everyman to a generall rekenynge.	*reckoning (judgment)*
	Gyve audyens and here what he wyll saye.	*Listen; hear*

God speketh [above]

GOD	I perceyve here in my majestye	
	How that all creatures be to me unkynde,	*unnatural*
	Lyvynge without drede in worldely prosperytye;	
25	Of ghostly syght the people be so blynde,	*spiritual*
	Drowned in synne, they know me not for ther God.	

[Translation of Dutch *Elckerlijc* continued]

At first God Almighty speaks thus:

GOD I see from my throne above / that all that is of human kind / lives without fear of God, ignorant.
/ I see the people so blinded / [5] by sin, that they don't recognize me as God.

Opten aertschen scat sijn si versot,
Dien hebben si voer Gode vercoren,
Ende mi vergheten, die hier te voren
Die doot heb geleden doer tsmenschen profijt.
10   Och Hovaerdie, die Ghiericheyt ende Nijt,
Metten vij Dootsonden vermoghen,
Hoe sidi ter werelt nu voert ghetoghen.
Want mits der vij Dootsonden gemeen
Es op ghedaen; des ick in ween
15   Ben seker met alder hemelscher scaren.
Dye vij Duechden, dye machtich waren,
Sijn alle verdreven ende verjaecht,
Want donnosel heeft mij seer gheclaecht.
Elckerlijc leeft nu buyten sorghen;
20   Nochtan en weten si ghenen morghen.
Ick sie wel hoe ic tvolc meer spare,
Hoet meer arghert van jare te jare.
Al dat op wast arghert voert.
Daer om wil ic nu, als behoert,
25   Rekenninghe van Elckerlijc ontfaen.
Want liet ic dye werelt dus langhe staen
In desen leven, in deser tempeesten,
Tvolc souden werden argher dan beesten
Ende souden noch deen den anderen eten.
30   Mijn puer ghelove is al vergheten,
Dat ic hem selven gheboot te houden,
Het cranct, het dwijnt, het staet te couden;
Daer ic so minlijc om sterf die doot,
Ontsculdich, sonder bedwanc oft noot,
35   Om dat ick hoepte, dat si bi desen
Mijnder eewigher glorien ghebrukich souden wesen,
Daer icse seer toe hadde vercoren.
Nu vinde ick dattet als is verloren
Dat icse so costelic hadde ghemeent.
40   Hoe menich goet ic hem vry heb verleent
Uut mijnder ontfermherticheydens tresoor
Dat hem recht toe hoort. Nochtans sijnse soe door,
Ende verblent int aertsche goet,
Als dat justicie wercken moet
45   Aen Elckerlijc, die leeft so onvervaert.

They are enamored of worldly treasures, / which they have chosen over God, / and have forgotten me, who heretofore / had suffered death for the profit of man. / [10] O Pride, Avarice, and Envy, / powerful among the Seven Deadly Sins, / how you have progressed now in the world. / Because of the Seven Deadly Sins together / has my vengeance been awakened; therefore I weep / [15] with all the heavenly hosts. / The Seven Virtues, which were powerful, / are all driven out and chased away, / for the innocent one has sorely complained to me about it. / Everyman now lives without concern; / [20] still they

In worldely ryches is all theyr mynde;
They fere not my ryghtwysenes, that sharpe rod.   *fear; righteousness*
My lawe that I shewed whan I for them dyed
30 They forgot clene, and sheddynge of my blod so redde.   *entirely; blood*
I hanged bytwene two theves, it cannot be denyed;
To get them lyfe I suffrede to be deed;   *allowed [myself]; dead*
I heled theyr fete, with thornes hurt was my heed.   *feet; head*
I coulde do no more than I dyde truely,
35 And now I se the people do clene forsake me.
They use the Seven Deedly Synnes dampnable,
As Pryde, Covetyse, Wrathe, and Lechery   *Covetousness*
Now in the worlde be made commendable,
And thus they leve of aungeles, the hevenly company.   *depart from*
40 Everyman lyveth so after his owne pleasure,
And yet of theyr lyfe they be not sure.   *secure*
I se the more that I them forbere   *tolerate*
The worse they are from yere to yere.
All that lyveth apperyth faste;   *degenerates quickly*
45 Therfore I wyll in all the haste
Have a rekenynge of every mannes persone.
For and I leve the people thus alone   *if I leave*
In theyr lyfe and wycked tempestes,
Verely they wyll becume moche worse than bestes,   *Truly; beasts*
50 For now one wolde by envy another up ete;   *eat up*
Charytye they all do clene forgete.
I hoped well that Everyman
In my glorye shulde make his mansyon,
And therto I had them all electe.   *chosen*
55 But now I se that, lyke traytours dejecte,   *debased*
They thanke me not for the pleasure that I to them ment,   *meant*
Nor yet for theyr beynge that I them have lente.   *their existence*
I profered the people great multytude of mercy,
And fewe there be that asketh it hertely.   *sincerely*
60 They be so cumbred with worldly ryches   *encumbered*
That nedes on them I must do justyce   *necessarily*
On every man lyvynge without feare.

---

are not sure about tomorrow. / I see how the more I spare the people, / the worse it gets from year to year. / All that grows up becomes ever worse. / Therefore I will now, as it is fitting, / [25] have the reckoning of Everyman. / For if I let the world continue in such a state / in this way of life, in these tempests, / the people would become worse than beasts / and would devour each other. / [30] Pure belief in me, which is completely forgotten, / that which I myself commanded them to keep, / it weakens, it disappears, it gets cold; / for this I died the death out of love, / in innocence, out of my free will and without constraint, / [35] because I hoped that through this / they would enjoy my everlasting glory, / for which I had expressly chosen them. / Now I think that everything is lost, / though I loved them at such a price. / [40] How many goods have I freely lent them / out of the treasure of my mercy / that thus belong to them by right. However, they are so foolish, / and blinded by earthly goods, / that justice must be done / [45] on Everyman, who is living so without fear. /

Waer sidi, mijn Doot, die niemant en spaert?
Coemt hier! Hoort wat ic u sal vermonden.

DIE DOOT   Tuwen beveele in allen stonden,
Almachtich God! Segt u beheet.

God Spreect

GOD   Gaet hene tot Elckerlijc ghereet,
51   Ende segt hem van mijnen twegen saen
Dat hi een pelgrimagie moet gaen
Die niemant ter werelt en mach verbi,
Ende dat hi rekeninghe come doen mi
55   Sonder vertrec: dats mijn ghebot.

DIE DOOT   Het wert ghedaen, almachtich God.
Ick wil ter werelt gaen regneren;
Oeck sal ic rasschelijc, sonder cesseren,
Tot Elckerlijc gaen. Hi leeft so beestelic
60   Buten Gods vreese ende alte vleeslick.
Voer God aenbidt hi deertsche goet,
[Daer hy deeuwighe vreughde om derven moet]
Daer wilic tot hem gaen met snellen keere.
Hi coemt hier gaende. Help, God Heere.
65   Hoe luttel vermoet hi op mijn comen!
Ay, Elckerlijc, u wert saen benomen
Dat ghi houden waent seer vast.
Ghi sult staen tot swaren last
Voor Gode almachtich ende buten seghe.
70   Elckerlijc, waer sidi op weghe
Dus moey? Hebdi al Gods vergheten?

ELCKERLIJC   Waerbi vraechdijs?

DIE DOOT   Dit suldi wel weten,
Wilt na mi hooren te desen stonden.
Naerstich bin ic aen u ghesonden
75   Van Gode uut des Hemels pleyn.

ELCKERLIJC   Aen mij ghesonden?

Where are you, my Death, who no one spares? / Come here! Hear what I shall say to you. / **DEATH**
At your command at all times, / Almighty God! Say what you demand. / *God speaks* / [50] **GOD** Go
hence to Everyman at once, / and tell him immediately in my name / that he must set forth on a pilgrimage / which no one in the world can escape, / and that to me he shall come to make his reckoning
/ [55] without delay: that is my command. / **DEATH** It shall be accomplished, Almighty God. / I shall
go forth to reign in the world; / also I shall quickly, without delay, / go to Everyman. He lives so
beastly / [60] without fear of God and too fleshly. / He worships earthly goods above God, / for which

Where art thou, Deth, thou myghty messengere?

[*Enter Death*]

DEATH Almyghty God, I am here at your wyll
65   Your commaundemente to fulfyll.

GOD Go thou to Everyman
      And shew hym in my name
      A pylgrymage he must on hym take
      Which he in no wyse may escape,
70   And that he brynge with hym a sure rekenynge   *accurate account*
      Without delay or ony taryenge.   *any tarrying*

DEATH Lorde, I wyll in the worlde go ren over all   *run everywhere*
      And cruelly out serche bothe great and small.   *search out [all]*
      Everyman I wyll beset that lyveth beestly   *who lives*
75   Out of Goddes lawes and dredeth not foly.
      He that loveth ryches I wyll stryke with my darte
      His syght to blynde, and from Heven depart,   *to part (separate)*
      Excepte that almes dedes be his good frende,   *Unless*
      In Hell for to dwell, worlde without ende.

      [*Enter Everyman*]

80   Loo, yonder I se Everyman walkynge.
      Full lytell he thynketh on my cummynge.
      His mynde is on flesshely lustes and his treasure,
      And great payne it shall cause hym to endure
      Before the Lorde, Heven Kynge.
85   Everyman, stonde styll. Whether arte thou goynge   *Whither (Where)*
      Thus gayly? Hast thou thy Maker forget?

EVERYMAN Why askest thou?
      Woldest thou wete?   *[What] would you know*

DEATH Ye, syr, I wyll shew you.   *Yes*
90   In great hast I am sende to thee
      From God out of his majestyé.

EVERYMAN What, sende to me?

---

he will have to lack eternal joy. / There I shall go to him soon. / Here he comes walking. Help, Lord God. / [65] How little he anticipates my coming! / Oh, Everyman, you will soon lose / what you think you hold firmly. / You will stand with a heavy burden / and in misery before Almighty God. / [70] Everyman, where are you going / so beautifully dressed? Have you entirely forgotten God? / EVERYMAN Why do you ask? DEATH This you will certainly discover, / if you listen to me in this hour. / Urgently I have been sent to you / [75] by God from Heaven's plain. / EVERYMAN Sent to me?

DIE DOOT   Jae ick, certeyn!
       Al hebdi sijns vergheten, alst blijct,
       Hi peynst wel om u in sijn rijck,
79   Alsoe ick u sal voer oghen legghen.

ELCKERLIJC   Wat begheert God van my?

DIE DOOT   Dat sal ick di segghen:
81   Rekenninghe wilt hi van u ontfaen
       Sonder eenich verdrach.

ELCKERLIJC   Hoe sal ic dat verstaen?
       Rekeninghe? wat salt bedieden?

DIE DOOT   Al ghevet u vreemt, het moet ghescieden.
85   Oec moetti aen nemen sonder verdrach
       Een pelgrimagie, die niemant en mach
       Weder keeren in gheender manieren.
       Brengt u ghescriften ende u pampieren
       Met u, ende oversietse bedachtich,
90   Want ghi moet voer God Almachtich
       Rekeninghe doen, des seker sijt,
       Ende hoe ghi bestaet hebt uwen tijt,
       Van uwen wercken, goet ende quaet.
       Oeck en hoort hier gheen verlaet
95   Van dien. Als nu het moet gheschien.

ELCKERLIJC   Daer op ben ic nu al qualic versien
       Rekeninghe te doen, voer Gode bloot.
       Wie bistu bode?

DIE DOOT   Ick ben die Doot die niemand en spaert,
       Maer Elckerlijck sal, bi
99   Gods beveele, doen rekeninghe mi.

ELCKERLIJC   Och Doot, sidi mi soe bi,
       Als icker alder minst op moede.
       Doot, wildi van mi hebben goede?
       Duysent pont sal ic u gheven,
       Op dat ic behouden mach mijn leven
105   Ende doet mi een verdrach van desen.

DEATH Yes I was, certainly! / Although you have forgotten him, as it appears, / he thinks of you in his kingdom, / as I will explain to you. / [80] **EVERYMAN** What does God want from me? **DEATH** That I will tell you: / he wants to receive a reckoning from you / without any delay. **EVERYMAN** How am I to understand that? / Reckoning? What does that mean? / **DEATH** Although it may seem strange to you, it must be. / [85] Also, you must without delay undertake / a pilgrimage, from which no one is

DEATH Ye, certaynly.
          Though thou have forgete hym here,
95   He thynketh on thee in the hevenly spere   *sphere*
          As or we departe thou shall knowe.   *before (ere)*

EVERYMAN What desyreth God of me?

DEATH That shall I shewe thee:
          A rekenynge he wyll nedes have   *he must have*
100   Without lenger respyte.   *[any] longer*

EVERYMAN To gyve a rekenynge longer layser I crave.   *leisure (more time)*
          This blynde mater trubleth my wytte.   *difficult [to interpret]*

DEATH On thee thou must take a longe journey.
          Therfore thy boke of counte with thee thou brynge,   *account book*
105   For turne agayne thou cannot by no waye;   *return*
          And loke thou be sure of thy rekenynge,
          For before God shalte thou answere and shewe
          Thy many badde dedes and good but a fewe,
          How thou hast spente thy lyfe and in what wyse,
110   Before the chefe Lorde of Paradyse.
          Have ado that thou were in that waye,   *Have a care*
          For wete thou well thou shalte make none attournay.   *know; no one [your]*

EVERYMAN Full unredy I am suche rekenynge to gyve.
114   I knowe thee not; what messanger arte thou?

DEATH I am Dethe that no man dredeth,   *adequately fears*
          For every man I rest and none spareth,   *arrest*
          For it is Goddes commaundement
          That all to me sholde be obedyent.

EVERYMAN O, Deth, thou cummest whan I had thee leest in mynde.
120   In thy power it lyeth me to save.
          Yet of my good wyll I gyve thee yf ye wyll be kynde,   *goods (property)*
          Ye, a thousande pounde shalte thou have,
          And dyfferre this mater tyll another daye.   *If [you will] defer*

---

able to / return by any way or means. / Bring your writing and your papers / with you, and look them over carefully, / [90] for you must before God Almighty / give an account, be sure of that, / of how you have spent your time, / of your works, good and bad. / Also on this matter do not delay / [95] about that. Because it must be accounted now. / **EVERYMAN** I am hardly prepared just now / to give reckoning just for God alone. / Who are you, messenger? / **DEATH** I am Death, who does not spare anyone, / but Everyman shall, by / God's command, give reckoning to me. / [100] **EVERYMAN** Oh, Death, you are come so near to me / when I least expected it. / Death, do you want money from me? / I will give you a thousand pounds / so that I may retain my life / [105] and be released from this. /

DIE DOOT   Elckerlijc, dat en mach niet wesen.
                Ick en aensie goet, schat, noch have.
                Paeus, hertoghe, coninc, noch grave
                En spare ic niet nae Gods ghebieden.
110   Waer ic met schatte te verleeden,
                Ick creghe wel alder werelt goet.
                Nu houtet al met mi den voet,
                Oec en gheve ic uutstel noch verdrach.

ELCKERLIJC   Allendich, arm katijf, O wach!
115   Nu en weet ick mijns selfs ghenen raet
                Van rekeninghe te doen: mijn pampier
                Es so verwerret ende so beslet
                Ic en sier gheen mouwen toe gheset.
                So is mijn herte om desen in vaer.
120   Och mocht ic noch leven xij jaer,
                So soudic mijn ghescrifte exponeren
                Ende oversien. Wilt doch cesseren
                Als nu, lieve Doot, van wraken,
                Tot dat ic versien bin op die saken.
125   Dat bid ic u doer Gods ontfermen.

DIE DOOT   U en mach baten smeken oft kermen.
                Dus siet wat u staet te beghinnen.

ELCKERLIJC   Lieve Doot, een sake doet mi bekennen:
                Al yst dat ic dese vaert moet aengaen,
130   Soudic niet moghen wederkeeren saen,
                Als ic mijn rekeninghe hadde ghestelt?

DIE DOOT   Neen ghi, nemmermeer!

ELCKERLIJC   Almoghende Gods ghewelt,
                Wilt mijns ontfermen in deser noot!
                En soudic niemant, cleyn noch groot,
135   Daer moghen leyden, had ict te doene?

DIE DOOT   Jae ghi, waer yemant so koene
                Dat hi die vaert met u bestonde.

DEATH Everyman, that cannot be. / I am not moved by goods, treasure, or property. / Pope, duke, king, nor count / do I spare, after God's command. / [110] If I were to be tempted by treasures, / I would obtain all worldly goods. / Now everyone must dance with me, / so I give neither delay nor respite. / **EVERYMAN** Miserable, poor wretch, O woe! / [115] Now I do not see any way to avoid this / reckoning: my record / is so confused and in such disarray / that I see no way to set it straight. / Therefore my heart is in fear. / [120] Oh, if I might live another twelve years, / then I would set straight my records / and review them. Please do stop speaking / of punishment, dear Death, / until I am prepared for this business. / [125] This I implore you, by God's mercy. / **DEATH** Neither begging nor groaning

DEATH	Everyman, it may not be by no waye.	
125	I set not by golde, sylver, nor rychesse,	*am indifferent to; wealth*
	Ne by pope, emperoure, kynge, duke, ne prynces.	
	For and I wolde receyve geftes great	*For if; gifts*
	All the worlde I myght gete;	
	All my custome is clene contrary.	
130	I gyve thee no respyte; come hens and not tary.	*hence; [do] not delay*

EVERYMAN	Alas, shall I have no longer respyte?	
	I may saye Deth geveth no warnynge;	
	To thynke on thee it maketh my herte secke,	*sick*
	For all unredy is my boke of rekenynge.	
135	But twelve yere and I myght have abydynge,	*If; delay*
	My countynge boke I wolde make so clere	
	That my rekenynge I sholde not nede to fere.	*fear*
	Wherfore, Deth, I praye thee for Goddes mercy,	
	Spare me tyll I be provyded of remedy.	

DEATH	Thee avayleth not to crye, wepe, and praye,	*It profits you nothing*
141	But hast thee lyghtly that thou were gone the journaye	*nimbly*
	And prove thy frendes yf thou can,	*test*
	For wete you well the tyde abydeth no man,	*know; time waits for*
	And in the worlde eche lyvynge creature	
145	For Adams synne must dye of nature.	*in the course of nature*

EVERYMAN	Deth, yf I sholde this pylgrymage take	
	And my rekenynge surely make,	
	Shewe me, for saynt charyté,	*holy charity (God's love)*
	Sholde I not come agayne shortly?	

DEATH	No, Everyman, and thou be ones there,	*if; once*
151	Thou must nevermore come here,	
	Trust me veryly.	

EVERYMAN	Gracyous God in hye sete celestyall,	*high seat (throne)*
	Have mercy on me in this moost nede.	
155	Shall I have no company fro this vale terestyall	*earthly valley*
	Of myne aqueyntaunce that waye me to lede?	

DEATH	Ye, yf ony be so hardy	*any*
	That wolde go with thee and bere thee cumpany.	

---

will do you any good. / Therefore think what you should do. / **EVERYMAN** Dear Death, just let me know one thing: / though I must undertake this journey, / [130] could I not return soon / when I should have settled my reckoning? / **DEATH** No, never! **EVERYMAN** Almighty power of God, / have pity on me in this need! / May I take no one, high or low, / [135] along there, if I could manage? / **DEATH** Yes, if there were anyone so bold / that he dares to go that journey with you. /

Spoet u, want God, die alle gronde
Doersiet met sinen godliken oghen,
140   Begheert dat ghi voer hem coemt toghen
U rekenninghe van dat ghi hebt bedreven.
Wat meendi, dat u hier is ghegheven
Tleven op daerde ende tijtlijc goet?

ELCKERLIJC Ay lazen, dat waendick!

DIE DOOT   Hoe sidi aldus onvroet,
145   Elckerlijc, daer ghi hebt vijf sinnen,
Dat ghi soe onsuver sijt van sinnen
Ende ic so haestelijc come onversien.

ELCKERLIJC Allendich katijf, waer sal ic vlien,
Dat ic af quame deser groter sorghen?
150   Lieve Doot, verdraghet mi tot morghen,
Dat ic mi bespreken mach van desen.

DIE DOOT Dat en wil ic niet consenteren in desen,
Noch en doe icx niet in gheender tijt.
Ick slae den sulcken ter stont int crijt,
155   Sonder voer raet, met eenen slach.
Aldus bereyt u in desen dach.
Ick wil uut uwen oghen vertrecken.
Siet dat ghi u naerstelic gaet betrecken
Te segghen: "Nu coemt den dach
160   Die Elckerlijc niet voer bi en mach."

ELCKERLIJC Ay, Elckerlijc, wat dede ic ye gheboren?
Ick sie mijn leven al verloren,
Nu ic doen moet dese langhe vaert,
Daer ic so qualic teghen ben bewaert.
165   Ic en hebbe noyt goet bedreven,
Aldus heb ic seer luttel ghescreven.
Hoe sal ic mi excuseren int claer?
Ey lacen, ic woude dat ic nu niet en waer:
Dat waer mijnder sielen groot toeverlaet.
170   Waer mach ic nu soecken troost of raet?

Hurry up, because God, who sees into / all depths with his divine eyes, / [140] commands you to come before him to show / your account of what you have done. / What do you think, that life on earth / and worldly goods were just given to you? / **EVERYMAN** Alas, so I thought! **DEATH** How can you be so foolish, / [145] Everyman, you have five senses after all, / and are so impure inside, / never expecting that I come so hastily. / **EVERYMAN** Miserable wretch, where shall I flee, / that I might escape from this great distress? / [150] Dear Death, give me respite until tomorrow, / so that I can ponder on this. / **DEATH** That I will not allow, / nor will I ever do so at any time. / I can smite anyone at once in the

	Hye thee that thou were gone to Goddes magnyfycens	*Hurry*
160	Thy rekenynge to gyve before his presence.	
	What, wenest thou thy lyfe is gyven thee	*think*
	And thy wordely gooddes also?	*worldly*

EVERYMAN I had wende so, verely.   *thought*

DEATH Ney, nay, it was but lend thee,   *lent [to]*
165   For as sone as thou arte go   *gone (dead)*
      Another a whyle shall have it, and than go therfro   *go from it (lose it)*
      Even as thou hast done.
      Everyman, thou arte mad, that hast thy wyttes fyve
      And here on erth wyll not amende thy lyve,
170   For sodenly I do cume.

EVERYMAN Oo, wretched caytyfe, whether shall I flee   *rascal, whither*
      That I myght scape this endles sorow?   *escape*
      Now, gentyll Deth, spare me tyll tomorow   *noble Death*
      That I may amende me
175   With good advysemente.   *consideration*

DEATH Nay, therto I wyll not consent,
      Nor no man wyll I respyte,
      But to the harte sodenly I shall smyte
      Without any advysement.
180   And now out of syght I wyll me hye;   *hurry*
      Se thou make thee redy shortely,
      For thou mayst saye, "This is the day
      That no man lyvynge may scape awaye."   *escape away [from]*

      [*Exit Death*]

EVERYMAN Alas, I may well wepe with syghes depe.
185   Now have I no maner of cumpany
      To helpe me in my journey, and me to kepe,   *look after*
      And also my wrytynge is full unredy.   *account [book]*
      How shall I do now, for to excuse me?
      I wolde to God I had never be gete: *been conceived (born)*
190   To my soule a great profyte it had be,   *been*
      For now I fere paynes huge and great.   *fear*

---

ring, / [155] without warning, with one stroke. / Therefore prepare yourself, even today. / I shall depart from your sight. / See that you seriously begin / to say: "Now comes the day / that Everyman cannot avoid." / **EVERYMAN** Oh, Everyman, why was I ever born? / I see my life already lost / now that I must take this long journey / for which I am so badly prepared. / [165] I have never done any good; / thus very little has been written down. / How shall I justify myself clearly? / Alas, I now wish that I did not exist: / that would be to my soul a great comfort. / [170] Where might I now seek help or counsel? /

God die Heere, die alle dinc voersiet,
Dat ic veel claghe, ten helpt niet.
Den tijt gaet verre, tes nae noene.
Ay lasen, wat staet mi nu te doene?
175 Wien mocht ic claghen dese sake?
Laet sien, oft ic mijn Gheselscap sprake
Ende leyde hem te voren om mede te trecken,
Soudt hijt mi ontseggen? Neen hi, ick wane:
Wi hebben ter werelt in onsen daghen
180 So groten vrientscap tsamen gedraghen;
Want ic betrou hem alder duecht.
Ick sien, des bin ic rechts verhuecht.
Oec wil ic hem toe spreken sonder verdrach.
Goeden dach, Gheselscap!

GHESELSCAP   Elckerlijc, goeden dach
185 Moet u Gode gheven ende ghesonde!
Hoe siedi dus deerlic doet mi orconde:
Hebdi yet sonderlings dat u let?

ELCKERLIJC Jae ick, Gheselscap.

GHESELSCAP   Achermen, hoe sidi dus ontset?
Lieve Elckerlijc, ontdect mi uwen noot.
190 Ic blive u bi tot in die doot,
Op goet gheselscap ende trou ghesworen.

ELCKERLIJC Ghi segt wel, Gheselscap, want tes verloren!

GHESELSCAP Ick moet al weten u druc, u lijden:
Een mensche mocht druc uut u snijden.
195 Waer u mesdaen, ic helpt u wreken,
Al soudicker bliven doot ghesteken
Ende ict wiste te voren claer.

ELCKERLIJC Danc hebt, Gheselscap.

Lord God, who foresees all things, / it helps me not so to complain. / Time is passing quickly, it is after noon. / Alas, what am I to do now? / [175] To whom might I complain concerning this matter? / Let's see, if I first spoke to my Fellowship / and propose to him to come with me, / would he refuse it? No, I think: / in our days in the world we have had / [180] such great friendship together; / so I anticipate all blessings from him. / I see him, which really makes me happy. / I will talk to him without delay. / Good day, Fellowship! **FELLOWSHIP** Everyman, a good day / [185] may God give you, and health! / How sad you look; tell me: / is there something special that bothers you? / **EVERYMAN** Yes, Fellowship. **FELLOWSHIP** Poor Fellow, why are you so upset? / Dear Everyman, tell me about your distress. / [190] I will stay with you until death, / because of the good friendship and loyalty that we

The tyme passeth. Lorde, helpe, that all wrought,   *help [me], who created all*
For though I mourne it avaleth nought.   *it does not help*
The day passeth, and is almost ago: *gone*
195   I wot not well what to do.   *know*
        To whome were I best my complante to make?
        What and I to Felawshyp therof spake   *What if*
        And shewed hym of this sodayne chaunce,   *[bad] fortune*
        For in hym is all myne affyaunce.   *trust*
200   We have in the worlde so many a daye
        Be good frendes in sporte and playe.   *Been*

            [*Enter Fellowship*]

        I se hym yonder cartaynely.   *certainly*
        I truste that he wyll bere me cumpany;
        Therfore to hym wyll I speke to ease my sorow.
205   Well met, good Felawshyp, and good morowe.

            Felawshyp speketh

FELLOWSHIP   Everyman, good morowe, by this daye.
        Syr, why lokest thou so pyteously?
        If anythynge be amys, I pray thee me saye   *amiss (wrong); pray that you tell me*
        That I may helpe to remedy.

EVERYMAN   Ye, good Felawshyp, ye,   *Yes*
211   I am in greate jeopardé.

FELLOWSHIP   My true frende, shew to me your mynde.
        I wyll not forsake thee unto my lyves ende   *life's*
214   In the way of good cumpany.

EVERYMAN   That is well spoken and lovyngly.

FELLOWSHIP   Syr, I must nedes know your hevynes.   *depressed mental state*
        I have pytye to se you in any destresse.
        If any have you wronged, ye shall revenged be,   *have wronged you*
        Though I on the grounde be slayne for thee,   *[battle]ground*
220   Though that I knowe before that I shulde dye.   *prior to that*

EVERYMAN   Veryly, Felawshyp, gramercy.   *thank you*

---

have sworn! / **EVERYMAN** Well said, Fellowship, for all is lost! / **FELLOWSHIP** I must know all your pain and suffering: / "It is so thick you could cut it with a knife." / [195] If any harm were done to you, I will help you to avenge it, / even if I would be stabbed to death / and I knew it clearly in advance. / **EVERYMAN** Thank you, Fellowship.

GHESELSCAP   Ghenen danck een haer.
        Daer by segt mi u doghen.

ELCKERLIJC   Gheselle, oft ick u leyde voer oghen
201   Ende u dien last viel te swaer,
        Dan soude ic mi meer bedroeven daer.
        Maer ghi segt wel; God moets u lonen.

GHESELSCAP   Way, ic meynet, al sonder honen.

ELCKERLIJC   Ghi segt wel, boven screve.
205a   Ic en vant noyt anders aen u dan trouwe.

GHESELSCAP   So en suldi oeck nemmermeer!

ELCKERLIJC   God loons u ende ons Vrouwe.
        Gheselle, ghi hebt mi wat verhaecht.

GHESELSCAP   Elckerlijc, en sijt niet versaecht.
209   Ick gae met u, al waert in die Helle.

ELCKERLIJC   Ghi spreect als een gheselle.
        Ic sal u dancken, als ic best kan.

GHESELSCAP   Daer en is gheen dancken aen.
        Diet niet en dade in wercken aenschijn,
        Hi en waer niet waert gheselle te sijn.
215   Daer om wilt mi uwen last ontdecken
        Als ghetrouwe vrient.

ELCKERLIJC   Ick salt u vertrecken
        Hier nu seker, al sonder veysen.
        Mi es bevolen dat ic moet reysen
        Een grote vaert, hardt ende stranghe.
220   Oec moet ic rekeninge doen bi bedwange
        Voer den hoochsten Coninc almachtich.
        Nu bid ic u dat ghi zijt bedachtich
        Mede te gaen, so ghi hebt beloeft.

GHESELSCAP   Dats wel blikelijc:
225   Die ghelofte houdic van waerden.
        Mer soudic sulcken reyse aenvaerden
        Om beden wille, mi souts verdrieten.

FELLOWSHIP No thanks at all. / Therefore tell me your grief. / [200] **EVERYMAN** Fellow, if I should make it clear / and the burden is too heavy for you, / then I would be more distressed. / But you say well; may God reward you. / **FELLOWSHIP** Well, I am serious, that is no lie. / [205] **EVERYMAN** You speak well, certainly. / [205a] I have never found anything but loyalty in you. / **FELLOWSHIP** And you

FELLOWSHIP Tusshe, be thy thankes I set not a straw.   *by; do not care*
      Shewe me your grefe, and say no more.

EVERYMAN Yf I my herte shulde to you breke,   *reveal*
225   And than you to turne your mynde from me
      And wold not me comforte when you here me speke,   *hear*
      Than shulde I ten tymes soryer be.   *more sorry*

FELLOWSHIP Syr, I say as I wyll do in dede.   *in deed (in my actions)*

EVERYMAN Than be you a good frende at nede.
230   I have founde you true here before.

FELLOWSHIP And so ye shall evermore,
      For in fayth and thou go to Hell,   *if you*
      I wyll not forsake thee by the waye.

EVERYMAN Ye speke lyke a good frende; I beleve you well.
235   I shall deserve it and I maye.   *repay it if I can*

FELLOWSHIP I speke of no deservynge, by this daye,
      For he that wyll saye and nothynge do
      Is not worthy with good company to go.
      Therfore shew me the grefe of your mynde
240   As to your frende moste lovynge and kynde.

EVERYMAN I shall shewe you how it is:
      Commaunded I am to go a journaye,
      A longe waye, herde and daungerous,   *hard*
      And gyve a strayte counte without delaye   *exact account*
245   Before the hye juge Adonay.
      Wherfore, I pray you, bere me company,
      As ye have promysed, in this journaye.

FELLOWSHIP That is matter indede. Promyse is dutye,   *matter (allegation) requiring proof*
      But and I shulde take suche a vyage on me,   *But if; journey*
250   I know it well, it shulde be to my payne;

---

will never find differently! **EVERYMAN** May God and our Lady reward you for it. / Fellow, you have somewhat given me strength. / **FELLOWSHIP** Everyman, do not be faint of heart. / I will go with you, even if it might be to Hell. / [210] **EVERYMAN** You speak as a real fellow. / I will pay you back, as best I can. / **FELLOWSHIP** There is no need for thanks. / He who would not prove it by deeds / is not worthy to be a fellow. / [215] Therefore reveal to me your trouble / as a true friend. **EVERYMAN** I will tell you certainly / here now, in all seriousness. / I have been ordered that I must go / on a long journey, harsh and painful. / [220] Also, I must give a reckoning by command / before the highest King almighty. / Now I pray that you be inclined / to go with me, as you promised. / **FELLOWSHIP** It is quite obvious: / [225] the promise I consider binding. / But should I undertake such a journey / at your request, I would regret it. /

Ic soude van deser gheruchte verscieten.
Mer doch willen wi dbeste doen
230   Ende ons beraden.

ELCKERLIJC   Och hoort doch dit sermoen!
Seydi mi niet, had icx noot,
Mede te gaen tot inder hellen doot,
Oft in die Helle, had ict begaert?

GHESELSCAP   Dat soudic seker, maer sulc ghevaert
235   Es uut ghesteken, plats metten ronsten.
Om waer te seggen: oft wi die vaert begonsten,
Wanneer souden wij weder comen na desen?

ELCKERLIJC   Daer en is gheen weder keeren.

GHESELSCAP   So en wil icker niet wesen.
239   Wie heeft u die bootscap ghebracht?

ELCKERLIJC   Ay lazen, die Doot!

GHESELSCAP   Help, heylighe Gods crachte,
Heeft die Doot gheweest die bode?
Om al dat leven macht van Gode
En ghinc icker niet, mocht icx voerbi.

ELCKERLIJC   Ghi seydet mi nochtans toe.

GHESELSCAP   Dat kenne ick vry.
245   Waert te drincken een goet ghelaghe,
Ick ghinc met u totten daghe,
Oft waert ter kermissen buten der stede,
Oft daer die schone vrouwen waren.

ELCKERLIJC   Daer ghingdi wel mede.
Waert altoos met ghenuechten te gaen, soe waerdi bereet.

I would be frightened of this burden. / But let's think it over / [230] and do the best we can. **EVERY-MAN** Oh, just listen to this sermon! / Did you not say, if I had need of it, / to go with me into infernal death, / or into Hell, if I had desired it? / **FELLOWSHIP** That I certainly would, but such a journey / [235] is out of the question, honestly speaking. / To tell you the truth: if we set out on the journey, / when should we come back thereafter? / **EVERYMAN** There is no coming back. **FELLOWSHIP** Then I do not want to be there. / Who has brought the message to you? / [240] **EVERYMAN** Alas, Death! **FELLOWSHIP** Help, holy God almighty, / has Death been the messenger? / For no living creature / would I go if I could avoid it. / **EVERYMAN** But you promised. **FELLOWSHIP** That I frankly admit. /

Also it maketh me aferde certayne.   *afraid*
But let us take councell here as we can,
For your wordes wold feare a stronge man.   *make a strong man to be afraid*

EVERYMAN   Why, ye sayd yf I had nede
255   Ye wolde me never forsake, quycke ne deed,   *living or dead*
Though it were to Hell truely.

FELLOWSHIP   So I sayde, certeynly,
But suche pleasures be set asyde, the sothe to say,   *truth*
And also yf we toke suche a journay,
260   Whan shulde we agayne cume?

EVERYMAN   Nay, nyver agayne, tyll the Day of Dome.   *Judgment Day*

FELLOWSHIP   In fayth, than wyll not I cume there.
Who hath you these tydynges brought?

EVERYMAN   Indede, Deth was with me here.

FELLOWSHIP   Now, by God that all hath bought,   *purchased (redeemed)*
266   If Dethe were the messengere,
For no man that is lyvynge todaye
I wyll not go that lothesom journay,
269   Not for the father that begat me.

EVERYMAN   Ye promysed me otherwyse, pardé.   *by God*

FELLOWSHIP   I wot well I sayd so, truely,   *know*
And yet, yf thou wylte ete and drynke and make good chere
Or haunte to women, that lusty cumpany,
I wolde not forsake you whyle the daye is clere —
275   Truste me veryly.

EVERYMAN   Ye, therto ye wolde be redy
To go to myrthe, solace, and playe;
Your mynde to folye wyll soner aply   *apply*
Than to bere me cumpany in my longe journey.

---

[245] If it were for a serious bout of drinking, / I would go with you until the break of day, / or if it were to go to the fair, outside the city limits, / or to where the beautiful women would be. **EVERYMAN** You would surely go with me there. / If it were only to go out for pleasure, then you were compliant. /

Gheselscap   Hier en wil ic niet mede, God weet.
251   Maer woudi pelgrimagie gaen,
       Oft woudi yemant doot slaen,
       Ic hulpen ontslippen tot in die broock ende oec cloven ontween.

Elckerlijc   Och dat is een sober bescheen!
255   Gheselle, ghi wilt anders dan ick alst noot is.
       Gheselle, peyst om trouwe die groot is
       Die wi deen den anderen over menich jaer
       Beloeft hebben.

Gheselscap   Trou hier, trou daer:
259   Ic en wilder niet aen. Daer mede gesloten.

Elckerlijc   Noch bid ic, en hadt u niet verdroten,
       Doet mi uut gheleye, maect mi moet,
       Tot voer die poerte.

Gheselscap   Tjacob! Ic en sal niet eenen voet!
       Mer haddi ter werelt noch ghebleven,
       Ick en hadde u nemmermeer begheven.
265   Nu moet u Ons Lieve Here gheleyden.
       Ick wil van u scheyden.

Elckerlijc   Es dat ghescheyden
       Sonder omsien? Ay lazen, jaet!
       Nu sien ic wel: tes cranc toeverlaet,
       Tgheselscap, alst coemt ter noot.
270   Mer waer ic noch in weelden groot,
       So soudtmen met mi lachen alteenen.
       Mer lazen! Men wilt met mi niet weenen.
       Men seit: "In voerspoet vintmen vrient,
       Die ter noot niet zeer en dient."
275   Een ander hem castie bi desen.
       Waer wil ic nu troost soeckende wesen?

---

[250] **FELLOWSHIP** Here I will not go, God knows. / But if you wanted to go on a pilgrimage, / or if you wanted to slay somebody, / I would help you strip him to his pants and cleave him in two. / **EVERYMAN** Oh, that is a useless answer! / [255] Fellow, what you want differs completely from what I require now that the need arises. / Fellow, think about that great loyalty / that we to one another many years ago / have promised. **FELLOWSHIP** Loyalty here, loyalty there: / I do not wish it, case closed. / [260] **EVERYMAN** Nevertheless I beseech you, if it were not unpleasant for you, / give me courage, lead me out, take me / up to the gates. **FELLOWSHIP** Not one step, by St. James! / But if you had remained in the world, / I would not have forsaken you. / [265] Our Dear Lord may accompany you now. / I will depart from you. **EVERYMAN** Is that parting / without looking back? Alas, indeed! / Now I see well: it is a weak support, / Fellowship, when need arises. / [270] But if I still were in great prosperity, / people would be laughing with me all the time. / Alas! They will not weep with me. / They

FELLOWSHIP   Nay, in good faythe, I wyll not that waye.   *will not [go] that way*
281   But and thou wylte murdre or any man kyll,   *if you will*
           In that I wyll helpe thee with a good wyll.

EVERYMAN   O, that is a symple advyse indede.   *foolish advice*
           Gentyll felawe, helpe me in my necessytye.
285   We have loved longe and now I nede,   *am in need*
           And now gentyll Felawshyp, remembre me.   *noble*

FELLOWSHIP   Whether ye have loved me or no,
           By Saynt Johnn, I wyll not with thee go.

EVERYMAN   Yet, I pray thee, take the laboure and do so moche for me   *make the effort*
290   To brynge me forwarde, for saynt charyté,
           And comforte me tyll I come without the towne.   *to the outside of*

FELLOWSHIP   Nay, and thou wolde gyve me a new gowne,   *[even] if you would*
           I wyll not one fote with thee goo.   *foot*
           But and thou had taryed I wolde not a left thee so;   *if; tarried; would not have*
295   And as now God spede thee in thy journey,   *God [may]*
           For from thee I wyll departe as fast as I may.   *far*

EVERYMAN   Whether awaye, Felawshyp? Wylt thou forsake me?   *Whither (where)*

FELLOWSHIP   Ye, by my faye. To God I betake thee.   *faith; commit you*

EVERYMAN   Farwell, good Felawshyp, for thee my herte is sore.
300   Adewe, for I shall never se thee no more.

FELLOWSHIP   In fayth, Everyman, farwell now at the endynge.
           For you I wyll remembre that partynge is mournynge.

           [*Exit Fellowship*]

EVERYMAN   Alacke, shall we thus departe indede?   *separate*
           O Lady, helpe! Without ony more comforte,   *Virgin Mary; any*
305   Lo, Felawshyp forsaketh me in my moste nede.
           For helpe in this worlde whether shall I resorte?   *where shall I turn*
           Felawshyp here before with me wolde mery make,
           And now lytell sorowe for me doeth he take.   *feel*
           It is sayd, "In prosperyté men frendes may fynde
310   Whiche in adversytye be full unkynde."
           Now whether for socoure shall I flee
           Syth that Felawshyp hath forsaken me?   *Since*

---

say: "In prosperity one finds a friend / who in need is of little use." / [275] This should be a warning to others. / Where shall I look for help now? /

Ic weet wel: aen mijn Vrient ende Maghe.
Dien wil ic minen noot gaen claghen.
Al is mi mijn Gheselscap af ghegaen,
280   Si moeten mi doch ter noot bi staen.
Want men doet int ghemeen ghewach,
"Dattet bloet cruypet, daert niet wel gaen en mach."
Ic salt besoecken, op dat ic leve.
Waer sidi, Vrienden ende Maghe?

MAGHE   Hier zijn wi, neve,
285   Tuwen ghebode, stout ende koene.

NEVE   Elckerlijc, hebdi ons te doene?
Dat segt ons vry.

MAGHE   Ja, sonder verlaet.
Wi zijn tuwen besten, wat ghi bestaet.
Al woudi yemant doot slaen,
290   Wi helpen u daer toe.

NEVE   Want het moet alsoe staen,
Salment maechscap te recht orboren.

ELCKERLIJC   God die danc u, mijn vrienden vercoren.
Ick claghe u, met droevigher herten, mijn ghevaernis,
Dat ic ontboden bin, alsoot claer is,
295   Een verre pelgrimagie te gaen
Daer nemmermeer en is wederkeeren aen.
Daer moet ic rekeninge doen, die swaer is,
Voerden Heere, diet al openbaer is.

MAGHE   Waer af moetti rekeninghe doen?

ELCKERLIJC   Van mijnen wercken, om cort sermoen:
301   Hoe ic hier mijnen tijt heb versleten
Op aertrijc ende met sonden verbeten
Ende wat ic heb bedreven
Den tijt, gheleent ende niet ghegheven.

/ I know well: with my Friend and Kinsman. / I will go to them to complain of my distress. / Though my Fellowship has abandoned me, / [280] they will certainly stand by me in distress. / For as the saying usually goes, / "Blood is thicker than water." / I shall test this that I may live. / Where are you, Friends and Kinsman? **KINSMAN** We are here, cousin, / [285] at your service, bold and brave. / **COUSIN** Everyman, do you need us? / Tell us frankly. / **KINSMAN** Yes, without delay. / We'll take care of you, whatever you may undertake. / Even if you wished to kill someone, / [290] we would help you with it. **COUSIN** For so must it be, / if one truly practices the duties of kinship. / **EVERYMAN** May God reward

    To my kynnesmen I wyll truely,
    Prayenge them to helpe me in my necessytye.
315   I beleve that they wyll do soo,
    "For kynde wyll crepe where it may not go."   *kindred; walk*

      [*Enter Kindred and Cousin*]

    I wyll go saye, for yender I se them.   *assay (test); over there I see them [passing by]*
    Where be ye now, my frendes and kynnesmen?

KINDRED Here be we now at your commaundemente.
320   Cosyn, I praye you, shewe us your intente
    In ony wyse and do not spare.   *any; hold anything back*

COUSIN Ye, Everyman, and us to declare,   *to us*
    Yf ye be dysposed to go ony whether,   *anywhere*
    For wot ye well, we wyll lyve and dye togyther.   *know*

KINDRED In welthe and wo we wyll with you holde,   *happiness; hold [fast]*
326   For over his kynne a man may be bolde.   *For with; kinfolk*

EVERYMAN Gramercy, my frendes and kynnesmen kynde,
    Now shall I shew you the grefe of my mynde.
    I was commaunded by a messengere
330   That is an hye Kynges chefe offycere;
    He bad me go a pylgrymage to my payne,
    But I know well I shall never cume agayne.   *return*
    Also, I must gyve rekenynge strayte,   *precise*
    For I have a great enemy that hath me in wayte   *who is observing me*
335   Whiche intendeth me for to hyndre.

KINDRED What a counte is that whiche ye must rendre?   *an account*
    That wolde I knowe.

EVERYMAN Of all my workes I must shewe
    How I have lyved and my dayes spente,
340   Also of yll dedes that I have used
    In my tyme syth lyfe was me lente,   *since*
    And of all vertues that I have refused.

---

you, my dear friends. / I lament to you, with saddened heart, of my predicament, / that I have been commanded, as clearly as can be, / [295] to go on a far pilgrimage / from which there is no returning. / There I must give reckoning, which is hard, / before the Lord, to whom all is revealed. / **KINSMAN** What is it of which you must give a reckoning? / [300] **EVERYMAN** Of my works, to speak concisely: / how I have squandered my time here / on earth and wasted away in sins / and of what I have done / in that time, lent to me, not given. /

305   Hier wilt doch mede gaen, dat u die Almachtige God wil lonen,
       Ende helpt mijn rekeninghe verschoonen.
       So sal te minder werden mijn seer.

MAGHE Wat! daer mede te gaen?

NEVE   Way, schillet niet meer?
309   Voerwaer, ick heb een ander ghepeyst.

MAGHE Ic valle op mijn achterhielen!

NEVE   Ten docht niet gheveyst:
       Ic seynder mijnre maerten bli ende vry.
       Si gaet gaerne ter feesten.

MAGHE   Ick segghe oeck alsoe
       Ick soude verschieten int laetste.

ELCKERLIJC En wildi dan niet mede gaen?

NEVE   En laet niet haesten, beste.
315   Ten is tot gheenre feesten te gaen,
       Noch tot gheenre sollen!

ELCKERLIJC   Nu, om een eynde te knopen,
       Segt, wildi mede, sonder verlaet?

MAGHE Neve, ic neme uutstel, dach ende raet
319   Ende mijn ghenachte tot open tijde.

NEVE   Wi willen ons verblasen.

ELCKERLIJC   Hoe soude ick verbliden?
       Wat schoonder woerden men mi biet,
       Alst coemt ter noot, so eest al niet.
       Ay lazen! Hoe ist hier ghevaren!

---

[305] Just go with me, that the Almighty God may reward you, / and assist in clearing my reckoning. / My grief will be less. / **KINSMAN** What, go with you there? **COUSIN** Well, is that all that is the matter? / Truly, I thought it was something else. / [310] **KINSMAN** I am bowled over! **COUSIN** No use pretending: / happily and willingly I'll send my maid there. / She likes to go to parties. **KINSMAN** That is what I say, too. / [320] I would be frightened in the end. / **EVERYMAN** Will you then not go with me? **COUSIN** Don't go so fast, my dear. / It is not a matter of going to any party / or game! **EVERYMAN** Now, then, to make an end of it, / say, will you go with me, without delaying? / **KINSMAN** Cousin, I shall take counsel, a recess, a time-out, / and an adjournment until the appropriate time.

Therfore, I praye you, go thether with me
To helpe to make myne accounte, for saynt charytie.

COUSIN   What, to go thether, is that the matter?
346   Nay, Everyman, I had lever fast breed and water   *rather fast [on] bread*
         All this fyve yere and more.

EVERYMAN   Alas that ever I was borne,
           For now shall I never be mery
350   Yf that you forsake me.

KINDRED   A, syr, what? Ye be a mery man,   *You are*
          Take good herte to you and make no mone!   *heart; moan*
          But one thynge I warne you, by Saynt Anne:
354   As for me, ye shall go alone.

EVERYMAN   My cosyn, wyll you not with me go?

COUSIN   No, by Our Lady, I have the crampe in my to.   *toe*
         Trust not to me, for so God me spede,
         I wyll deceyve you in your moste nede.

KINDRED   It avayleth not us to tyse.   *to attempt to entice us*
360   Ye shall have my mayde, with all my herte;
          She loveth to go to festes, there to be nyce   *feasts; be wanton*
          And to daunce and abrode to sterte.   *to go gadding*
          I wyll gyve her leve to helpe you in that jurnaye,
          If that you and she may agree.

EVERYMAN   Now shewe me the very effecte of your mynde;   *state*
366   Wyll you go with me, or abyde behynde?

KINDRED   Abyde behynde? Ye, that wyll I and I may;   *if I may*
          Therfore farwell tyll another daye!

          [*Exit Kindred*]

EVERYMAN   How shulde I be mery or gladde,
370   For fayre promyses men to me do make,
           But whan I have moste nede, they me forsake.
           I am deceyved, that maketh me sad.

/ [320] COUSIN We would like some breathing room. EVERYMAN How could I be glad? / Whatever
fine words they offer me, / when the need comes, then it is all for naught. / Alas! How things have
transpired here! /

NEVE   Elckerlijc, neve, God moet u bewaren.
325   Ic en wil niet mede, opt platte gheseyt.
            Oec heb ic uutstaende te rekenen wat,
            Daer bin ic noch qualic op versien.
            Dus blive ic hier.

ELCKERLIJC   Dat mach wel zijn.
            Tfy, Elckerlijc, hebdi u verlaten
330   Op u Mage? Die hem so vroemlijc vermaten,
            Laten u bliven in desen dangier.
            Siet, oftmense jaechde van hier.
            Ick sie: men spreect wel metten monde,
            Buyten der daet, uut geveynsden gronde.
335   Dan seghen si: "Neve, ghebreect u yet,
            Ic ben tuwen besten." Tes seker nyet.
            Ende des ghelijc seyt tGheselscap; doch
            Tes al zoringhe ende bedroch.
            Die wil, macher hem toe verlaten.
340   Waer mocht ic mi nu henen saten?
            Hier is verloren langhe ghebleven.
            Wat vrienden sullen mi nu troost geven?
            Daer coemt mi wat nieus inne:
            Ic heb aen mijn Goet geleyt grote minne.
345   Wilde mij dat helpen tot mijnen orboren,
            So en had ict noch niet al verloren.
            Ic heb op hem noch alle mijn troost.
            O Heere, diet al sal doemen,
            Wilt u gracie op mi ontsluyten.
350   Waer sidi, mijn Goet?

TGOET   Ick legghe hier in muten
            Versockelt, vermost, als ghi mi siet,
            Vertast, vervuylt. Ic en kan mi niet
            Verporren, also ic ben tsamen gesmoert.
            Wat wildi mi hebben?

ELCKERLIJC   Coemt rasch hier voert,
355   Lichtelic, Goet, ende laet u sien.
            Ghi moet mi beraden.

COUSIN Everyman, cousin, may God keep you. / [325] To be blunt, I do not want to come with you. / I also have some business to settle, / for which I still am badly prepared. / Hence I shall stay here. / EVERYMAN So be it. / Fie, Everyman, did you place trust / [330] in your Kinsman? The ones who promised so bravely / leave you in this misery. / Look, it is as if someone has driven them from here. / I see: one speaks well with one's mouth / out of hypocrisy, but without the deed. / [335] Then they

COUSIN   Cosyn Everyman, farwell now,
               For verely I wyll not go with you.
375   Also of my owne, an unredy rekenynge   *remain behind*
               I have to accounte; therfore I make taryenge.   *preserve you*
               Now God kepe thee, for now I go.

               [*Exit Cousin*]

EVERYMAN   A, Jesus, is all cume hereto?
               Loo, fayre wordes maketh fooles fayne;   *glad*
380   They promyse, and nothynge wyll do certayne.
               My kynnesmen promysed me faythfully
               For to abyde with me stedfastly,
               And now fast awaye do they flee,
               Evyn so Felawshyp promysed me.
385   What frende were best me of to provyde?   *would be best*
               I lose my tyme here longer to abyde,
               Yet in my mynde a thynge there is.
               All my lyfe I have loved ryches.
               If that my Good now helpe me myght,
390   It wolde make my herte full lyght.
               I wyll speke to hym in this dystresse.
               Where arte thou, my Goodes and Ryches?

               [*Goods speaks*]

GOODS   Who calleth me? Everyman? What, hast thou haste?   *are you in a hurry*
               I lye here in corners trussed and pyled so hye,
395   And in chestes I am locked full fast,
               Also sacked in bagges, thou mayste se with thyne eye.
               I cannot stere, in packes low I lye.   *stir (move)*
               What wolde ye have? Lyghtly me saye.   *Quickly*

EVERYMAN   Cume hyther, Good, in all the hast thou may,   *haste*
400   For of councell I must desyre thee.

---

say: "Cousin, if you lack anything, / I am here for you." It surely is nothing. / And Fellowship says the
same thing; yet / it is all betrayal and deceit. / Whoever wishes may rely on it. / [340] Now where can
I turn? / Remaining here any longer is useless. / What friends would assist me now? / A new thought
comes to me: / I have given great love to my Goods. / [345] If that would assist me to my benefit, / I
would not have lost everything yet. / From him I still expect my comfort. / O Lord, who shall judge
all, / open thy grace to me. / [350] Where are you, my Goods? GOODS I lie here locked up, / neglect-
ed, mouldy, as you see me, / heaped up, filthy; I cannot / move, pressed as I am together. / What will
you have of me? EVERYMAN Come forward here immediately, / [355] quickly, Goods, and show
yourself. / You must help me.

TGOET   Wat rade sal u van mi gheschien?
    Hebdi ter werelt eenich letten,
    Dat sal ic u beteren.

ELCKERLIJC   Tes al een ander smette.
    Ten is niet ter werelt, wilt mi verstaen.
360 Ick bin ontboden daer ic moet gaen
    Een grote pelgrimagie, sonder verdrach.
    Oec moet ic, dat is mij tswaerste gelach,
    Rekeninghe doen voerden oversten Heere,
    Om dwelc ic troost aen u begheere.
365 Mits dien dat ic in kintschen tijden
    Hadde in u groot verblijden,
    Ende dat mijnen troest al aen u stoet.
    So bid ic u, mijn uutvercoren Goet,
    Dat ghi met mi gaet sonder cesseren.
370 Want ghi mocht mi licht voer Gode pureren,
    Want Tgoet kan suveren smetten claer.

TGOET Neen, Elckerlijc, ic mocht u letten daer.
    Ic en volghe niemant tot sulcker reisen.
    Ende al ghinghe ic mede, wilt peisen,
375 So soudi mijns te wors hebben grotelic,
    Bi redenen ic salt u segghen blotelijc:
    Ic heb zeer u pampier verweert.
    Want al u sinnen hebdi verteert
    Aen mi, dat mach u leet zijn.
380 Want u rekeninghe sal onghereet zijn
    Voer God Almachtich, mits minen scouwen.

ELCKERLIJC Dat mach mi wel berouwen,
    Als ict verantwoerden sal moeten strangelic.
    Op, ga wi, mede!

TGOET   Neen, ick bin onbrangelijc.
385 Aldus en volghe ic u niet een twint.

ELCKERLIJC Ay lazen! Ick heb u oeck ghemint
    Mijn leefdaghe tot opten tijt van nu.

TGOET Dat es een eewige verdomenis voer u:
    Mijn minne es contrarye des Hemels staten.

GOODS What counsel must you have from me? / If you have any need in the world, / I will set it right.
EVERYMAN Something entirely different troubles me. / It is not of this world, you understand. / [360]
I have been summoned to where I must go / on a long pilgrimage, without delay. / I must also give,
and that is the worst of all, / a reckoning before the Lord most high, / for which I seek help from you.

GOODS   Syr, and ye in the worlde have trouble or adversyté,   *if you*
        Than can I helpe you to remedye shortely.

EVERYMAN   It is another dysease that grevyth me;   *trouble; makes me grieve*
        In this worlde it is not, I tell soo.
405   I am sende for another waye to go
        To gyve a strayte accounte generall   *precise account of everything*
        Before the hyghest Jupyter of all.
        And all my lyfe I have had joye and pleasure in thee;   *Since*
        Therfore, I praye thee, go with me,
410   For peraventure thou mayest before God Almyghty
        My rekenynge helpe to clene and puryfye,
        For it is sayd ever amonge
        That "money maketh all ryght that is wronge."

GOODS   Nay, Everyman, I synge another songe.
415   I folow no man in suche vyages,   *journeys*
        For and I wente with thee   *if I*
        Thou shuldest fare moche the worse for me;
        For bycause on me thou dyde set thy mynde,   *Since*
        Thy rekenynge I have made blotted and blynde   *illegible*
420   That thyne accounte thou cannot make truely,
        And that haste thou for the love of me.   *have you*

EVERYMAN   That wolde greve me full sore   *grieve*
        Whan I shulde cum to that ferefull answere;
        Up, let us go thyther togyther.

GOODS   Nay, not so; I am to bryttell, I may not endure;   *too weak*
426   I wyll folow no man one fote, be thou sure.

EVERYMAN   Alas, I have thee loved and had great pleasure
        All my lyfe dayes on good and treasure.   *(i.e., material things)*

GOODS   That is to thy dampnacyon without lesynge,   *lying*
430   For my love is contrary to the love everlastynge.

/ [365] Because, since my younger years, / I had great joy in you, / and my confidence rests entirely on you. / So I beg you, my dear Goods, / that you go with me without hesitation. / [370] For you could easily clear me before God, / since Goods can erase stains completely. / **GOODS** No, Everyman, I might hinder you there. / I follow no man on such a journey. / And even if I went with you, do consider, / [375] you would fare far worse off because of me, / for reasons I will tell you candidly: / I have botched your accounts terribly. / Since you have given your whole being / to me, for this you may be sorry. / [380] Your reckoning will not be in order / before God Almighty, through my fault. / **EVERYMAN** That I may well repent / when I must give a strict account. / Up, let's go together. **GOODS** No, I will not budge. / [385] Therefore I simply will not follow you. / **EVERYMAN** Alas! But I have loved you / my whole life until the present day. / **GOODS** That means everlasting damnation for you: / love for me is contrary to Heaven. /

390   Maer haddi mi gemint bi maten
        Ende van mi ghedeylt den armen,
        So en dorfstu nu niet karmen,
        Noch staen bedroeft, dat u nu swaer is.

ELCKERLIJC Ay lazen, God! Ic ken dat waer is.

TGOET Waendi dat ic u bin?

ELCKERLIJC   Ick hadt ghemeent.

TGOET Swijcht! Ic en bin mer u gheleent
        Van Gode; hy proeft, claer alst is voer oghen,
        Hoe ghi sult in weelden poghen.
        Die menighe blijft bi mi verloren,
400   Meer dan behouden, weet dat te voren.
        Waendi dat ic u sal volgen, Elckerlijc,
        Van deser werelt? Neen ic, sekerlijc!

ELCKERLIJC Dat waende ic claerlijc, om dat ic u oyt hadde so lief.

TGOET Daer om: tGoet kenne ic der sielen dief.
405   Als ghi nu van hier zijt, dat en mach niet lieghen:
        Soe wil ic eenen anderen bedrieghen,
        Ghelijc ic dede voer uwen tijt.

ELCKERLIJC Och valsche Goet, vermaledijt!
        Hoe hebdi mi in u net bevaen,
410   Verrader Gods!

TGOET   Ghi hebt dat al u selven ghedaen,
        Dat mi lief es te deser tijt.
        Ic moet daer om lachen!

ELCKERLIJC   Sidi dies verblijt,
        Om dat ghi mi van Gode hebt beroeft?
        Hi is sot, die eenich goet gheloeft.
415   Dat mach ic, Elckerlijc, wel beclaghen.
        En wildi dan niet mede?

---

[390] But had you loved me in moderation / and shared me with the poor, / then you would not need to whine now, / nor be sad, which is painful for you. / **EVERYMAN** Alas, God! I admit that this is true. / [395] **GOODS** Think you that I am yours? **EVERYMAN** I had thought so. **GOODS** Be silent! I am only lent to you / by God; he tests, it is as clear as day, / how you shall handle your wealth. / Many more are lost because of me / [400] than are saved, be sure of that. / Do you think that I will follow you, Everyman, / from this world? No, certainly not! / **EVERYMAN** That I thought for sure, because

But yf thou had me loved moderately durynge   *during [your lifetime]*
As to the poore to gyve parte of me,
Than shouldest thou not in this doloure be,
Nor in this great sorow and care.

EVERYMAN   Lo now, I was deceyved or I was ware,   *before I was ready*
436   And all I may wyte my spendynge of tyme.   *blame my wasting*

GOODS   What, wenest thou that I am thyne?   *think*

EVERYMAN   I had wente so.   *thought*

GOODS   Nay, Everyman, I say noo.
440   As for a whyle I was lente thee,
          A season thou haste had me in prosperytye.
          My condycyon is mannes soule to kyll;
          Yf I save one, a thousande I do spyll.   *destroy*
          Wenest thou that I wyll folowe thee   *Think*
445   From this worlde, nay, verely?   *truly*

EVERYMAN   I had wende otherwyse.

GOODS   Therfore to thy soule Good is a thefe,
          For whan thou arte deed this is my guyse: *practice*
          Another to deceyve in the same wyse
450   As I have done thee, and al to his soules reprefe.   *shame*

EVERYMAN   O false Good, cursed thou be,
          Thou traytour to God, thou hast deceyved me
          And caught me in thy snare!

GOODS   Mary, thou brought thyselfe in care,
455   Whereof I am gladde;
          I must nedes laugh. I cannot be sad.

EVERYMAN   A, Good, thou hast had longe my hartely love.   *sincere*
          I gave thee that whiche shulde be the Lordes above,
          But wylt thou not go with me indede,
460   I praye thee, truthe to saye?

I always loved you so much. / **GOODS** Therefore I know Goods as a thief of souls. / [405] When you are gone from here now, this is for sure: / I will deceive another, / just as I did one prior to your time. / **EVERYMAN** Oh false Goods, curse on you! / How you have caught me in your net, [410] traitor to God! **GOODS** You have done it all to yourself, / which amuses me now. / It makes me laugh! **EVERYMAN** You are pleased about this, / that you have robbed me of God? / He is foolish who puts his trust in any goods. / [415] This I, Everyman, may well lament. / Will you not go with me then?

TGOET   Ey seker, neen ick!

ELCKERLIJC   Och, wien sal ict dan claghen
            Mede te gaen in desen groten last?
            Eerst had ic op mijn Gheselscap ghepast;
            Die seydt mi schoen toe menichfout,
420   Mer achter na sloech hi mi niet hout.
            Daer vandic dattet al was bedroch.
            Doen ghinc ic tot minen Maghen noch;
            Die seydent mi toe, claer als ghelas.
            Ten eynde vandic als ghedwas.
425   Doen wert ic dencken op mijn Goet,
            Daer ic aen leyde minen moet.
            Dat en gaf mi troest noch raet
            Dan dattet Goet in verdoemenis staet.
            Dies ic mi selven wel mach bespuwen.
430   Tfy, Elckerlijc, u mach wel gruwen.
            Hoe deerlic mach ic u versmaden!
            Heere God, wie sal mi nu beraden,
            Daer ic noch bi werde verhuecht?
            Niemant bat dan mijn Duecht.
435   Maer lazen! Si is so teer van leden,
            Ic meen, si niet connen en sou vander steden.
            Och, en sal ic haer nyet toe dorren spreken?
            Wil ic? Neen ick. Ick sal nochtan.
            Tvare alst mach, ic moeter henen.
440   Waer sidi, mijn Duecht?

DUECHT   Ick ligghe hier al verdwenen
            Te bedde, vercrepelt ende al ontset.
            Ick en kan gheroeren niet een let.
            So hebdi mi ghevoecht met uwen misdaden.
            Wat is u ghelieven?

ELCKERLIJC   Ghi moet mi beraden,
445   Want icx noot heb, tot mijnder vromen.

GOODS Absolutely not! **EVERYMAN** Oh, to whom shall I then complain / to go with me in this great need? / First I had counted on Fellowship, / who repeatedly made me beautiful promises / [420] but who was not faithful to me afterwards. / Then I found that it was all deception. / Thereafter I went also to my kinsmen, / who promised it to me clear as glass. / In the end I found it to be all foolishness. / [425] Then I started to think of my Goods, / on which I had set my heart. / That gave me neither help nor counsel / other than that Goods stands damned. / Therefore I may as well spit at myself. / [430] Fie, Everyman, you may indeed shudder, / how thoroughly can I despise you! / Lord God, who will

GOODS No, so God me spede. *prosper*
Therfore farwell and have good daye.

[*Exit Goods*]

EVERYMAN O, to whome shall I make my mone *complaint*
For to go with me in that hevy journaye? *sorrowful*
465 Fyrst Felawshyp — he sayd he wolde with me go.
His wordes were very plesaunte and gaye,
But afterwarde he lefte me alone.
Than spake I to my kynnysmen all in despayre,
And also they gave me wordes fayre.
470 They lacked no fayre spekynge,
But all forsake me in the endynge.
Than wente I to my Goodes that I loved best
In hope to have cumforte, but there had I leest,
For my Goodes sharpely dyd me tell
475 That he bryngeth many into Hell.
Than of myselfe I was ashamed,
And so I am worthy to be blamed:
Thus may I well myselfe hate.
Of whome shall I now councell take?
480 I thynke that I shall never spede *succeed (prosper)*
Tyll that I go to my Good Dede,
But, alas, she is so weke *weak*
That she can nother go nor speke. *neither walk*
Yet wyll I ventre on her now. *test her*
485 My Good Dedes, where be you?

[*Good Deeds is unable to rise*]

GOOD DEEDS Here I ly, colde in the grounde.
Thy synnes have me so sore bounde
That I cannot stere. *stir (move)*

EVERYMAN O, Good Dedes, I stonde in feare.
490 I must you praye of councell, *advice*
For helpe now shulde cum ryght well. *be right welcome*

---

now help me / by which I yet would be happy? / No one better than my Virtue. / [435] But, alas! She is so weak in her limbs / I think she would not be able to move from her place. / Ah, shall I not then dare to speak to her? / Shall I? No! I shall nevertheless. / Fare as it may, I must go there. / [440] Where are you, my Virtue? **VIRTUE** I lie here all withered / in bed, paralyzed and entirely dejected. / I cannot move a limb. / Thus you have made me with your misdeeds. / What do you desire? **EVERYMAN** You must help me, / [445] for I need it to my benefit. /

DUECHT Elckerlijc, ic heb wel vernomen
Dat ghi ter rekeninghen sijt ghedaecht
Voer den oversten Heere.

ELCKERLIJC   Och, dat si u gheclaecht.
Ic come u bidden uuttermaten
450   Dat ghi daer met mi gaet.

DUECHT   Al mocht mi al die werelt baten,
Ick en konst niet alleen ghestaen.

ELCKERLIJC Ay lazen! Sidi so cranck?

DUECHT   Dit hebdi mi al ghedaen.
Haddi mi volcomelijc ghevoecht,
Ic sou u rekeninghe, die nu onreyn is,
455   Gesuvert hebben, des u siel in weyn is.
Siet u ghescrifte ende uwe wercken,
Hoe dat si hier legghen.

ELCKERLIJC   Gods cracht wil mi stercken!
Men siet hier een letter niet die reyn es.
Is dit al mijn ghescrifte?

DUECHT   Seker ick meens.
460   Dat moechdi sien aen mijn ghesonde.

ELCKERLIJC Mijn waerde Duecht, uut goeden gronde,
Ic bid u troost mi tot mijnen orboren,
Oft ic bin eewelijc verloren.
Want Geselscap, Vrient, Maghe, ende Goet
465   Sijn mi af ghegaen, in rechter oetmoet:
Helpt mi mijn rekeninghe sluyten hier voer den hoochsten Heere.

DUECHT Elckerlijc, ghi deert mi seere.
Ick sou u helpen, waer icx machtich.

ELCKERLIJC Duecht, soudi mi wel beraden?

DUECHT   Dies bin ick bedachtich,
470   Hoe wel ic niet en mach vander steden.

VIRTUE Everyman, I have understood / that you have been summoned to a reckoning / before the Lord who is over all things. EVERYMAN Oh, about that I want to complain to you. / I come to ask you urgently / [450] that you go there with me. VIRTUE Even if I might gain all the world, / I could not stand by myself. / EVERYMAN Alas! Are you so feeble? VIRTUE You have done all this to me. / Had

GOOD DEEDS Everyman, I have understandynge
That thou arte somoned, a counte to make   *an account*
Before Messyas of Jerusalem Kynge.   *[the] Messiah*
495 And you do by me, that journaye with you will I take.   *If you follow my advice*

EVERYMAN Therfore I cum to you, my mone to make.   *complaint*
I pray thee to go with me.

GOOD DEEDS I wolde full fayne, but I cannot stonde verely.   *gladly; stand*

EVERYMAN Why, is there anythinge on you fall?   *has anything happened to you*

GOOD DEEDS Ye, syr, I may thanke you of all.
501 Yf ye had perfytely chered me,   *supported (nurtured)*
Your boke of accounte full redy now had be.   *been*
Loke the bokes of your workes and deeds eke,   *Look [at]; also*
Beholde how they lye under the fete
505 To your soules hevynes.   *sorrow*

EVERYMAN Our Lorde Jesus helpe me,
For one letter herein can I not se.

GOOD DEEDS There is a blynde rekenynge in tyme of dystresse.   *obscured (illegible)*

EVERYMAN Good Dedes, I praye you helpe me in this nede,
510 Or els I am forever damned indede.
Therfore helpe me to make my rekenynge
Before the Redemer of all thynge
That Kynge is and was and ever shall.   *shall [be]*

GOOD DEEDS Everyman, I am sory of your fall,
515 And fayne wolde I helpe you and I were able.   *gladly; if I were*

EVERYMAN Good Dedes, your councell I pray you gyve me.

GOOD DEEDS That shall I do verely,
Though that on my fete I may not go.

---

you altogether gone along with me, / I would have cleansed your reckoning, / [455] which now is unclean, and that is why your soul is so sad. / Look at your records and your deeds, / how they lie here. **EVERYMAN** May God's power strengthen me! / One does not see a single letter that is clean. / Are these all my records? **VIRTUE** I certainly believe so. / [460] You can see that from the state of my health. / **EVERYMAN** My dear Virtue, from the goodness of your heart, / I beg you to help me to my advantage, / or I will be lost forever. / For Fellowship, Friend, Kinsman, and Goods / [465] have forsaken me, in just humility / help me to balance my reckoning here before the highest Lord. / **VIRTUE** Everyman, you have my deepest sympathy. / I would help you, if I were able. / **EVERYMAN** Virtue, would you indeed advise me? **VIRTUE** This I intend, / [470] though I cannot move from my place. /

Noch heb ic een suster, die sal gaen mede.
Kennisse heetse, die u leyden sal
Ende wijsen hoemen u bereyden sal
474   Te trecken ter rekeninghe, die fel es.

KENNISSE Elckerlijc, ick sal u bewaren.

ELCKERLIJC   Ick waen, mi nu wel es.
Ick ben eens deels ghepayt van desen.
Gods lof moeter in gheeert wesen.

DUECHT Als si u gheleyt heeft sonder letten
Daer ghi u suveren sult van smetten,
480   Dan sal ic gesont werden ende comen u bij
Ende gaen ter rekeningen als Duecht mit di,
Om te helpen zommeren tot uwer vruecht
Voerden oversten Heere.

ELCKERLIJC   Danck hebt, uutvercoren Duecht!
Ick bin ghetroost boven maten
485   Op u suete woerden.

KENNISSE   Nu gaen wi ons saten
Tot Biechten. Si es een suver rivier,
Sy sal u pureren.

ELCKERLIJC   Uut reyner bestier
So gaen wi tot daer. Ic bids u beyden:
Waer woent Biechte?

KENNISSE   Int Huys der Salicheden.
490   Daer sullen wijse vinden, soudic meenen.

ELCKERLIJC Ons Here God wil ons gracie verleenen
Tot haer, die ons vertroosten moet.

KENNISSE Elckerlijc, dit is Biechte; valt haer te voet.
Sy es voer Gode lief ende waert.

Yet I have a sister who will go with you. / Her name is Knowledge, who will guide you / and show you another who will prepare you / for setting forth to the reckoning, which is severe. / [475] **KNOWLEDGE** Everyman, I shall protect you. **EVERYMAN** I believe I feel better now. / I am a little reassured by this. / In this God may be praised. / **VIRTUE** When without delay she has led you / where you shall cleanse yourself from stains, / [480] then I shall receive my health and help you / and go with you to the reckoning as Virtue, / to help you with your accounting, to your joy, / before the Lord who is over all.

I have a syster that shall with you also
520   Called Knowlege, which shall with you abyde
       To helpe you to make that dredfull rekenynge.   *terror-inspiring*

       [*Enter Knowledge*]

KNOWLEDGE   Everyman, I wyll go with thee and be thy guyde
       In thy moste nede to go by thy syde.

EVERYMAN   In good condycyon I am now in everythynge,
525   And am holy contente with this good thynge,   *wholly*
       Thankyd be God my Creature.   *Creator*

GOOD DEEDS   And whan she hath brought thee there
       Where thou shalte heale thee of thy smarte,   *pain*
       Than go thou with thy rekenynge and thy Good Dedes togyther
530   For to make thee joyfull at harte
       Before the blessyd Trynytye.

EVERYMAN   My Good Dedes, I thanke thee hartfully;   *sincerely*
       I am well contente certaynly
       With your wordes swete.

KNOWLEDGE   Now go we thether lovyngly   *thither*
536   To Confessyon, that clensynge ryvere.

EVERYMAN   For joye I wepe; I wolde we were there.
       But I praye you to instructe me by intelleccyon,
       Where dwellyth that holy man Confessyon?

KNOWLEDGE   In the House of Salvacyon
541   We shall fynde hym in that place
       That shall us cumforte, by Goddes grace.

       [*Everyman is led to Confession*]

       Loo, this is Confessyon. Knele downe and aske mercy,
       For he is in good conceyte with God Almyghty.   *esteem*

EVERYMAN Thank you, Virtue, my favorite! / I am extremely comforted / [485] by your sweet words.
KNOWLEDGE Now we will go / to Confession. She is a clear river, / she will cleanse you. EVERYMAN
With pure intent / we shall go there. Pray, tell me, both of you: / where does Confession live?
KNOWLEDGE In the House of Salvation. / [490] There we shall find her, I think. / EVERYMAN Our
Lord may grant us grace / with her, who may comfort us. / KNOWLEDGE Everyman, this is Confession;
fall at her feet. / She is very dear and precious to God. /

ELCKERLIJC O gloriose bloome, diet al verclaert
496   Ende doncker smetten doet vergaen,
             Ick knyele voer u. Wilt mi dwaen
             Van mijnen sonden. In u aenscouwen
             Ick coem met Kennisse te mijnen behouwe,
500   Bedroeft van herten ende seer versaecht,
             Want ic ben vander Doot ghedaecht
             Te gaen een pelgrimagie, die groot is.
             Oec moet ic rekening doen, die bloot is,
             Voor hem, die doersiet gronde.
505   Nu bid ic, Biechte, moeder van ghesonde:
             Verclaert mijn brieven, want Duecht seer onghesont is.

BIECHTE Elckerlijc, u lijden mi wel kont is.
             Om dat ghi mit Kennisse tot mi sijt comen,
             So sal ic u troesten tuwer vromen.
510   Oec sal ic u gheven een juweelken rene,
             Dat Penitencie heet alleene.
             Daer suldi u lichaem mede termijnen
             Met abstinencie ende met pijnen.
             Hout daer, siet die gheesselen puere:
515   Dats Penitencie, strang ende suere.
             Peyst dat Ons Here oeck was gheslaghen
             Met geesselen, dat hi woude verdraghen
             Recht voer sijn pelgrimagie stranghe.
             Kennisse, hout hem in desen ganghe;
520   So sal sijn Duecht werden spoedich.
             Ende emmer hoept aen Gode oetmoedich,
             Want u tijt varinck eynden sal.
             Bidt hem ghenade; dit suldi vinden al,
             Ende orboert die harde knopen altijt.
525   Kennisse, siet dat ghi bi hem sijt
             Als hi tot Penitencien keert.

KENNISSE Gaerne, Biechte.

ELCKERLIJC   God si hier in Gheeert!
             Nu wil ic mijn penitencie beghinnen,
             Want dlicht heeft mi verlicht van binnen,
530   Al sijn dese knopen strenghe ende hardt.

---

[495] **EVERYMAN** O glorious flower, that shines / and makes dark stains to disappear, / I kneel before you. Do cleanse me / of my sins. Into your sight / I come with Knowledge for my salvation, / [500] sad of heart and very afraid, / because I have been summoned by Death / to go on a great pilgrimage. / Also, I must give a reckoning, as is clear, / before him, who sees through all reasoning. / [505] Now I pray, Confession, mother of health: / cleanse my records, for Virtue is very ill. / **CONFESSION** Every-

EVERYMAN [*Spoken kneeling*]
545 O gloryous fountayne that all unclennes doth clarify, *make clear (cleanse)*
 Wasshe from me the spottes of vyces unclene
 That on me no synne may be sene.
 I cum with Knowlege for my redempcyon,
 Repent with herte and full contrycyon, *sincerity*
550 For I am commaunded a pylgrymage to take
 And great accountes before God to make.
 Now I praye you, Shryfte, mother of Salvacyon, *Confession*
 Helpe my Good Dedes, for my petyous exclamacyon.

CONFESSION I know your sorowe well, Everyman,
555 Bycause with Knowlege ye cum to me.
 I wyll you comforte as well as I can,
 And a precyous jewell I wyll gyve thee
 Called Penaunce, voyder of adversytye. *remover*
 Therwith shall your body chastysed be
560 With abstynence and perseveraunce in Goddes servyce.
 Here shall you receyve that scurge of me
 Whiche is Penaunce stronge that ye must endure
 To remembre thy Savyoure was scurged for thee
 With sharpe scurges and suffered it pacyently.
565 So must thou or thou scape that paynful pylgrymage. *before you escape*
 Knowlege, kepe hym in this vyage, *journey*
 And by that tyme Good Dedes wyll be with thee,
 But in any wyse be sure of mercy,
 For your tyme draweth fast, and ye wyll saved be. *is coming quickly when ye*
570 Aske God mercy, and he wyll graunte truely.
 Whan with the scurge of Penaunce man doth hym bynde, *himself*
 The Oyle of Forgyvenes than shall he fynde.

EVERYMAN Thanked be God for his gracyous werke,
 For now I wyll my penaunce begynne;
575 This hath rejoysed and lyghted my herte, *made me happy*
 Though the knottes be paynfull and harde within. *knots [of rope scourge]*

---

man, to me your suffering is well known. / Because you have come to me with Knowledge, / I will help you to your advantage. / [510] Also, I will give you a perfect jewel, / that is simply called Penance. / With that you shall chastise your body / with abstinence and suffering. / Imagine, see the pure scourge: / [515] that is Penance, hard and sour. / Remember that Our Lord also was beaten / with scourges, which he willed to endure, / just before his cruel pilgrimage. / Knowledge, keep him on this path; / [520] then his Virtue will become strong. / And always humbly hope in God, / for your time will soon end. / Beg mercy of him; you will find it fully, / and always use the hard knots of the scourge. / [525] Knowledge, see that you are beside him / when he turns to Penance. **KNOWLEDGE** Gladly, Confession. **EVERYMAN** God be honored in this! / Now I shall begin my penance, / for the light has enlightened me within, / [530] though these knots are harsh and hard. /

KENNISSE Elckerlijc, hoe suer dat u wert,
          Siet dat ghi u penitencie volstaet.
          Ick, Kennisse, sal u gheven raet,
534   Dat ghi u rekeninghe sult tonen bloot.

ELCKERLIJC O levende Leven! O hemels Broot!
          O Wech der waerheyt! O Godlic Wesen,
          Die neder quam uut sijns Vaders schoot
          In een suver Maecht gheresen,
          Om dat ghi Elckerlijc wout ghenesen,
540   Die Adam onterfde bi Yeven rade.
          O Heylighe Triniteyt uut ghelesen,
          Wilt mi vergheven mijn mesdade,
          Want ic begheer aen u ghenade.

          O godlijc Tresoer! O coninclijc Saet!
545   O alder werelt Toeverlaet,
          Specie der engelen sonder versaden,
          Spiegel der vruecht daert al aen staet,
          Wiens licht Hemel ende aerde beslaet,
          Hoor mijn roepen, al yst te spade.
550   Mijn bede wilt inden troen ontfaen.
          Al bin ic sondich, mesdadich ende quaet,
          Scrijft mi int boeck des Hemels blade,
          Want ic begheer aen u ghenade.

          O Maria, moeder des hemels Almachtich,
555   Staet mi ter noot bi voordachtich
          Dat mi die Viant niet en verlade.
          Want nakende is mi die Doot crachtich.
          Bidt voer mi dijnen Sone voerdachtich,
          So dat ic mach gaen inden rechten pade
560   Daer die wegen niet en sijn onrachtich.
          Maect mi uwes Kints rijc delachtich,
          So dat ic in sijn Passie bade,
          Want ic begheer aen u ghenade.

          Kennisse, gheeft mi die gheselen bi vramen,
565   Die penitencie hieten bi namen.
          Ic salt beghinnen, God geefs mi gracie.

KNOWLEDGE Everyman, however unpleasant it may become for you, / see that you carry out your penance. / I, Knowledge, will help you, / so that you can openly show your reckoning. / [535] **EVERYMAN** O living Life! O heavenly Bread! / O Way of truth! O Divine Being, / who descended from his Father's bosom, / coming down into a pure Maid, / because you wanted to heal Everyman, / [540] whom Adam disinherited by Eve's counsel. / O Holy Trinity of supreme excellence, / do forgive me my misdeeds, / for I seek mercy from you. / O divine Treasure! O royal Seed! / [545] O Refuge for

KNOWLEDGE   Everyman, your penaunce loke that ye fulfyll
               What payne that ever it to you be,
               And Knowlege wyll gyve you councell at wyll
580   How your accounte ye shall make clerely.

EVERYMAN   O eternall God! O hevenly Fygure!   *Form*
               O Way of ryghtwysenes, O goodly Vysyon   *righteousness*
               Whiche descended downe in a vyrgyn pure
               Bycause he wolde Everyman to redeme
585   Whiche Adam forfeyted by his dysobedyens.
               O blessyd Godhede electe and hye devyne,   *exalted*
               Forgyve me my grevous offence.
               Here I crye thee mercy in this presence,
               O ghostly Treasure, O Raunsomer and Redemer,   *spiritual*
590   Of all the worlde hope and conductor,   *guide*
               Myrrour of joye and Founder of mercy,
               Whiche enlumyneth Heven and erth therby,   *illumines*
               Here my clamorous complaynte, though it late be,   *Hear*
               Receyve my prayers unworthy of thy benygnyté,   *graciousness*
595   Though I be a synner moste abhomynable.
               Yet let my name be wryten in Moyses table.
               O Mary, pray to the Maker of all thynge
               Me for to helpe at my endynge,
               And save me from the power of my enemy,
600   For Deth assayleth me strongly,
               And, Lady, that I may by meane of thy prayer   *by the instrumentality*
               Of thy Sonnes glory to be partetaker.
               By the meanes of his Passyon, I it crave,   *Suffering; beg*
               I beseche you helpe my soule to save.

               [*Everyman rises*]

605   Knowlege, gyve me the scorge of penaunce;
               My flesshe therwith shall gyve acqueyntaunce.   *be acquainted*
               I wyll now begynne, yf God gyve me grace.

---

the entire world, / ever-replenishing Food of angels, / Mirror of joy on whom all depends, / whose light covers Heaven and earth, / hear my crying, even if it may be too late. / [550] Receive my prayer at the throne. / Though I am sinful, wicked and evil, / write me in the book of Heaven, / for I seek mercy from you. / O Mary, mother of the heavenly Almighty, / [555] stand carefully by me in need / so that the Devil does not overpower me. / For mighty Death is approaching me. / Pray diligently for me to your Son, / so that I am able to walk on the right path / [560] where the ways are not crooked. / Impart to me the kingdom of your Child, / so that I can bathe in his Passion, / for I desire mercy from you. / Knowledge, give me the scourge for my own good / [565] which by name is called Penance. / I shall begin, may God favor me. /

Kennisse Elckerlijc, God gheve u spacie!
      So ghevicx u inden naem ons Heeren,
569   Daer ghi ter rekeninghe moet keeren.

[Elckerlijc] Inden naem des Vaders ende des Soens, mede
      Des Heylige Gheest, inder Drievuldichede,
      Beghin ic mijn penitencie te doen.
      Neemt, lichaem, voer dat ghie waert so scoen
      Mij te bringhen inden wech der plaghen.
575   Daer om moetti nu sijn gheslagen.
      Ghi hebbes wel verdient ghewarich.
      Ay broeders, waer soe mochti
      Door penitencie waen tseghen dat ghi u pelgrimaige moet gaen,
      Die Elckerlijc moet nemen aen.

Duecht God danc, ic beghin nu wel te gaen,
581   Want Elckerlijc heeft mi ghenesen.
      Dies wil ic eewich bi hem wesen.
      Oeck sal ic sijn weldaet clareren; dies wil ic bi hem gaen te tijde.

Kennisse Elckerlijc, sijt vro ende blijde:
585   U Weldaet coemt, nu sijt verhuecht!

Elckerlijc Wie maecht sijn, Kennisse?

Kennisse   Het is u Duecht,
      Gans ende ghesont op die beene.

Elckerlijc Van blijscappen ic weene.
      Nu wil ic meer slaen dan te voren.

Duecht Elckerlijc, pelgrijm uutvercoren,
591   Ghebenedijt sidi, sone der victorien,
      Want u is nakende dlicht der glorien.
      Ghi hebt mi ghemaect al ghesont;
      Des sal ic u bi bliven teewigher stont.
595   God sal dijnre ontfermen, hebt goet betrouwen.

Elckerlijc Welcoem, Duecht, mijn oghen douwen
      In rechter oetmoedigher blijscap soet.

Knowledge Everyman, may God give you time! / I will give [the scourge] to you in the name of our Lord, / to whom you must come to give reckoning. / [570] **Everyman** In the name of the Father and the Son, also / the Holy Ghost, in the Trinity, / I am beginning to do my penance. / Take this, body, for the fact that you were so reckless / to lead me on the path of disaster. / [575] Therefore now you must be beaten. / You have truly indeed deserved it. / Oh, brothers, you must truly / wade through penance in preparation for the time you go on your pilgrimage, / which Everyman must undertake.

KNOWLEDGE   Everyman, God gyve you tyme and space.   *opportunity*
    Thus I bequethe you in the handes of our Savyoure,   *hand you over into*
610   Now may you make your rekenynge sure.

EVERYMAN   In the name of the Holy Trynyté,
    My body sore punysshyd shal be.

    [*Everyman scourges himself*]

    Take this, body, for the synne of the flesshe!
    Also thou delytest to go gaye and fresshe,
615   And in the waye of dampnacyon thou dyd me brynge;
    Therfore suffre nowe strokes and punysshenge.
    Now of penaunce I wyll wade the water clere
    To save me from Hell and from the fyre.

    [*Good Deeds rises and stands*]

GOOD DEEDS   I thanke God now I can walke and go.
620   I am delyvered of my sekenesse and wo;
    Therfore with Everyman I wyll go and not spare.
    His good workes I wyll helpe hym to declare.

KNOWLEDGE   Now, Everyman, be mery and gladde.
    Your Good Dedes do come, ye may not be sadde.
625   Now is your Good Dedes hole and sounde,   *whole*
    Goynge upryght upon the grounde.   *Walking*

EVERYMAN   My herte is lyght and shall be evermore;
    Now wyll I smyte faster than I dyd before.

GOOD DEEDS   Everyman, pylgrym, my specyall frende,
630   Blessyd be thou without ende,
    For thee is prepared the eternall glory.
    Ye have me made hole and sounde;   *whole*
    Therfore I wyll abyde with thee in every stounde.   *remain with; moment [of trial]*

EVERYMAN   Welcume, my Good Dedes, now I here thy voyce.   *now [that] I hear*
635   I wepe for very swetenes of love.

/ [580] **VIRTUE** Thank God, I am beginning to feel well, / because Everyman has healed me. / Therefore I shall be with him forever. / I shall also testify to his good deeds; for that I shall go with him at once. / **KNOWLEDGE** Everyman, be happy and pleased: / [585] Good Deeds comes to you, now rejoice! / **EVERYMAN** Who can it be, Knowledge? **KNOWLEDGE** It is your Virtue, / whole and healthy on her legs. / **EVERYMAN** I weep for joy. / Now I will strike harder than before. / [590] **VIRTUE** Everyman, elect pilgrim, / blessed be you, son of victory, / for the light of glory is coming to you. / You have made me completely healthy; / therefore I shall remain with you forever. / [595] God will have mercy on you, be assured. / **EVERYMAN** Welcome, Virtue, my eyes grow misty / in truly humble, sweet joy. /

KENNISSE En slaet niet meer, hebt goeden moet:
      God siet u leven inden throone.
600   Doet aen dit cleet tuwen loone.
      Het is met uwen tranen bevloeyt,
      Dus draechtet vrij, onghemoeyt;
      Oft anders soudijt voor Gode gemissen.

ELCKERLIJC Hoe heet dit cleet?

KENNISSE   Tcleet van Berouwenissen.
605   Het sal Gode alte wel behaghen.

DUECHT Elckerlijc, wilt dat cleet aendraghen,
      Want Kennisse hevet u aenghedaen.

ELCKERLIJC Soe wil ic Berouwenisse ontfaen,
      Om dat God dit cleet heeft so weert.
610   Nu willen wi gaen onverveert.
      Duecht, hebdi ons rekeninghe claer?

DUECHT Jae ic, Elckerlijc.

ELCKERLIJC   So en heb ic ghenen vaer.
      Op vrienden, en wilt van mi niet sceyden.

KENNISSE Neen wi, Elckerlijc.

DUECHT   Ghi moet noch met u leyden
615   Drie personen van groter macht.

ELCKERLIJC Wie souden si wesen?

DUECHT   Wijsheyt ende u Cracht;
      U Scoonheit en mach niet achter bliven.

KENNISSE Noch moetti hebben sonder becliven
619   U Vijf Sinnen als u beraders.

KNOWLEDGE Strike no more, cheer up: / God on his throne sees you live. / [600] Put on this garment as your reward. / It is soaked with your tears, / so wear it freely, in perseverance; / otherwise you would be lacking before God. / **EVERYMAN** What is this garment called? **KNOWLEDGE** The garment of Remorse. / [605] It will please God very much. / **VIRTUE** Everyman, wear this garment / that Knowledge has put on you. / **EVERYMAN** Thus I will receive Remorse, / because God values this garment so highly. / [610] Now let us go without fear. / Virtue, have you our reckoning clear? / **VIRTUE** Yes, Everyman. / **EVERYMAN** Then I have no fear. / Let's go, friends, do not part from me. / **KNOWLEDGE** Not us, Everyman. **VIRTUE** You must take with you also / [615] three persons of great power. / **EVERY-**

KNOWLEDGE Be no more sad, but evermore rejoyce.
　　　　God seeth thy lyvynge in his trone above.   *way of life; throne*
　　　　Put on this garment to thy behove,   *benefit*
　　　　Whiche with your teres is now all wete,
640　　Lest before God it be unswete
　　　　Whan you to your journeyes ende cume shall.

EVERYMAN Gentyll Knowlege, what do ye it call?   *Noble*

KNOWLEDGE It is the garmente of Sorowe.
　　　　From payne it wyll you borow.   *save (protect)*
645　　Contrycyon it is
　　　　That getteth forgyvenes;
　　　　It pleasyth God passynge well.   *very well*

GOOD DEEDS Everyman, wyll you were it for your hele?   *wear; [soul's] health*

　　　　　　[*Everyman puts on the Garment of Contrition*]

EVERYMAN Now blessyd be Jesu, Maryes sonne,
650　　For now have I on true Contrycyon,   *have I put on*
　　　　And let us go now without taryenge.   *tarrying*
　　　　Good Dedes, have we clere oure rekenynge?

GOOD DEEDS Ye, indede, I have it here.

EVERYMAN Than I trust we nede not fere;   *fear*
655　　Now frendes, let us not parte in twayne.   *from each other*

KNOWLEDGE Nay, Everyman, that wyll we not, certayne.

GOOD DEEDS Yet must thou lede with thee   *bring with you*
　　　　Thre persones of great myght.

EVERYMAN Who shulde they be?

GOOD DEEDS Dyscressyon and Strengthe they hyght,   *are called*
661　　And thy Beautye may not abyde behynde.

KNOWLEDGE Also ye must call to mynde
　　　　Your Fyve Wyttes as for your councellers.

GOOD DEEDS You must have them redy at all houres.

MAN Who might they be? VIRTUE Prudence and your Strength; / your Beauty may not stay behind.
/ KNOWLEDGE You must also without delay have / [619] your Five Senses as your assistants. /

ELCKERLIJC Hoe soude icxse ghecrighen?

KENNISSE   Roepse alle gader.
          Si sullent hooren al sonder verdrach.

ELCKERLIJC Mijn vrienden, coemt alle op mijnen dach:
          Wijsheyt, Cracht, Scoonheyt, ende Vijf Sinnen!

CRACHT Hier sijn wi alle tot uwer minnen.
625   Wat wildi van ons hebben ghedaen?

DUECHT Dat ghi met Elckerlijc wilt gaen
          Sijn pelgrimagie helpen volbringhen.
          [Want hi gedaecht is ter rekeningen]
          Voor Gode te comen onghelet.
630   Siet oft ghi mede wilt.

SCHOONHEYT   Wie willen alle met,
          Tsijnre hulpen ende tsijnen rade.

VROETSCAP Dat willen wi certeyn.

ELCKERLIJC   O Almoghende God, ghenade!
          U love ic dat ic dus heb ghebracht
          Vroescap, Scoonheyt, Vijf Sinnen, ende Cracht,
635   Ende mijn Duecht met Kennisse claer.
          Nu heb ic gheselscap te wille daer.
          Ic en geerder niet meer te minen verdoene.

CRACHT Ick blive u bi, stout ende koene,
          Al waert te gaen in eenen strijt.

VIJF SINNEN Ende ic, al waert die werelt wijt,
641   Ic en scheyde van u in gheenre noot.

SCHOONHEYT So en sal ic oeck tot in die doot,
          Comer af datter afcomen mach!

VROETSCAP Elckerlijc, wes ic u doe ghewach:
645   Gaet voersienich ende al met staden.

---

[620] **EVERYMAN** How should I obtain them? **KNOWLEDGE** Call all of them. / They will hear all about it without delay. / **EVERYMAN** My friends, come all on this my day: / Prudence, Strength, Beauty, and Five Senses! / **STRENGTH** Here we are, all of us, at your service. [625] What do you want us to do? / **VIRTUE** That you will go with Everyman / to help him complete his pilgrimage. / For he has been summoned to come / at once before God for a reckoning. [630] See if you want to come with him. **BEAUTY** We all want to go with him / to help and assist him. / **PRUDENCE** That we will, certainly. /

EVERYMAN   How shall I get them hyther?

KNOWLEDGE   You must call them all togyther,
667   And they wyll here you incontynent.   *hear; immediately*

EVERYMAN   My frendes, cume hyder and be present,
         Dyscressyon, Strength, my Fyve Wyttes, and Beautye.

         [*Enter Discretion, Strength, Five Wits, and Beauty*]

BEAUTY   Here at your wyll we be redy.
671   What wolde ye that we shalde do?

GOOD DEEDS   That ye wold with Everyman go
         And helpe hym in his pylgrymage.
         Advyse you: wyll ye with hym or not in that vyage?   *Think; journey*

STRENGTH   We wyll brynge hym all thether
676   To his helpe and cumforte, ye may beleve me.

DISCRETION   So wyll we go with hym all togyther.

EVERYMAN   Almyghty God, loved may thou be!   *praised*
         I gyve thee laude that I have hether brought   *praise; hither*
680   Strength, Dyscressyon, Beauté, and Fyve Wyttes, lac I nought,   *lack; nothing*
         And my Good Dedes, with Knowlege clere;
         All be in cumpany at my wyll here.   *my command*
         I desyre no more to my besynes.   *business (purpose)*

STRENGTH   And I, Strength, wyll stonde by you in destresse,
685   Thoughe thou woldest in batayll fyght on the grounde.   *[battle] ground*

FIVE WITS   And though it were throughe the worlde rounde,
         We wyll not departe for swete nor soure.

BEAUTY   No more wyll I unto dethes houre,
         Whatsoever therof befall.

DISCRETION   Everyman, advyse you fyrst of all,   *consider*
691   Go with a good advysement and delyberycyon.   *consideration*

EVERYMAN O Almighty God, mercy! / I praise you that I thus have brought along / Prudence, Beauty, Five Senses, and Strength, / [635] and my Virtue and clear Knowledge. / Now I have company here that pleases me. / I have no more wishes for myself. / STRENGTH I shall remain with you, bold and brave, / even if it meant going into battle. / [640] FIVE SENSES Me too, even if we had to go the whole wide world, / I shall not part from you in any distress. / BEAUTY Neither shall I until death, / come of it what may! / PRUDENCE Everyman, what I wanted to tell you: / [645] go with foresight, calm and collected. /

Wi sullen u alle duecht raden
Ende sullen u helpen wel bestieren.

ELCKERLIJC Dit sijn vrienden die niet en faelgieren;
Dat lone hem God, die hemelsche Vader.
650   Nu hoort, mijn vrienden, alle gader:
Ick wil gaen stellen mijn testament
Voor u allen hier in present.
In caritaten ende in rechter oetmoede
Deel ic den armen van mijnen goede
655   Deen helft, ende dander helft daer nae
Ghevick daer si schuldich is te gaen.
Dit te doen ic den Viant nu te schanden,
Om los te gaen uut sinen handen,
Nae mijn leven in desen daghe.

KENNISSE Elckerlijc, hoort wat ick ghewaghe:
661   Gaet totten priesterliken staet
Ende siet dat ghi van hem ontfaet
Tsacrament ende Olijs mede.
Dan keert hier weder tot deser stede.
665   Wi sullen alle nae u verbeyden.

VIJF SINNEN Jae, Elckerlijc, gaet u bereyden.
Ten is keyser, coninc, hertoghe, of grave
Die van Gode hebben alsulcken gave,
Als die minste priester doet alleene.
670   Van alden sacramenten reene
Draecht hi den slotel, al doer bereyt
Tot des menschen salicheyt,
Die ons God teender medecijne
Gaf uuter herten sijne,
675   Hier in desen aertschen leven.
Die Heylighe Sacramenten seven:
Doopsel, Vormsel, Priesterscap goet,
Ende tSacrament, God vleesch ende bloet,
Huwelic ende tHeylich Olyzel met,
680   Dit zijn die seven onbesmet:
Sacramenten van groter waerden.

We will counsel you in all good things / and guide you in the right direction. / **EVERYMAN** These are friends who do not fail; / may God, the heavenly Father, reward them. / [650] Now listen, all my friends: / I am going to make my will / before all of you here present. / In charity and genuine humility / I distribute to the poor of my goods / [655] one half, and the other half thereafter / I assign to where by right it should go. / I do this now to shame the Devil, / to get out of his claws, / when my life ends this day. / [660] **KNOWLEDGE** Everyman, listen to what I say: / go to the priesthood / and see that you from them receive / the Sacrament and the Chrism. / Then come back to this place here. /

We all gyve you vertuous monycyon   *virtuous admonition*
That all shall be well.

EVERYMAN   My frendes, herken what I wyll tell:
695   I pray God rewarde you in his hevenly spere.   *sphere*
Now herken all that be here,
For I wyll make my testament   *will (legal document)*
Here before you all presente.
In almes half my good I wyll gyve with my handes twayne
700   In the waye of charytye with good entent,
And the other halfe styll shall remane
In quyet to be returned there it ought to be.   *bequest; where*
This I do in despyte of the fende of Hell
To go quyte out of his parell   *To be released from peril (of the fiend)*
705   Ever after and this daye.

KNOWLEDGE   Everyman, herken what I saye:
Go to Pryesthode, I you advyse,
And receyve of hym in ony wyse   *any*
The Holy Sacramente and Oyntment togyther;   *Extreme Unction*
710   Than shortely se ye turne agayne hyder.   *see that you return here*
We wyll all abyde you here.   *wait for you*

FIVE WITS   Ye, Everyman, hye you that ye redy were.   *hurry; will be ready*
Theyr is no emperour, kynge, duke, ne baron
That of God hath commyssyon   *authority*
715   As hath the leest pryest in the worlde beynge,   *most lowly priest*
For of the blessyd Sacramentes pure and benygne   *benign*
He bereth the keyes and therof hathe he cure.   *charge (care)*
For mannes redempcyon it is ever sure
Whiche God for our soules medycyne
720   Gave us out of his harte with great pyne   *pain*
Here in this transytory lyfe for thee and me.
The blessyd Sacramentes seven there be:
Baptym, Confyrmacyon, with Pryesthode good,   *Ordination*
And the Sacrament of Goddes precyous flesshe and blode;   *(i.e., Eucharist)*
725   Maryage, the holy Extreme Unccyon, and Penaunce.
These seven be good to have in remembraunce,
Gracyous Sacramentes of hye dyvynyté.

---

[665] We shall all wait for you. / **FIVE SENSES** Yes, Everyman, go prepare yourself. / There is no emperor, king, duke, or count / who has from God such a gift / as does the lowliest priest alone. / [670] Of all the pure sacraments / he has the key, always ready / for humankind's salvation, / which God for a medicine / gave us from out of his heart / [675] here, in this earthly life. / The Seven Holy Sacraments: / Baptism, Confirmation, Holy Orders, / and the Eucharist, God's flesh and blood, / Marriage and the Extreme Unction also: / [680] these are the seven unblemished: / Sacraments of great value. /

ELCKERLIJC Ic wil Gods lichaem minlic aenvaerden
      Ende oetmoedelijc totten priester gaen.

VIJF SINNEN Elckerlijc, dat is wel ghedaen.
685   God laet u met salicheden volbringhen!
      Die priester gaet boven alle dinghen:
      Si zijn die ons die Scriftueren leeren
      Ende den mensche van sonden keeren.
      God heeft hem meer machts gegheven
690   Dan den ynghelen int eewich leven.
      Want elc priester kan maken claer,
      Met vijf woerden opten outaer
      Inder Missen (des zijt vroet),
      Gods lichaem, warachtich vleesch ende bloet,
695   Ende handelt den Scepper tusscen zijn handen.
      Die priester bint ende ontbint alle banden
      Inden Hemel ende opter aerde.
      Och edel priester van groter waerde,
      Al custen wi u voetstappen, gi waret waert!
700   Wie van sonden troost begaert,
      Die en connen vinden gheen toeverlaet
      Dan aenden priesterliken staet.
      Dit heeft die Heere den priester gegheven,
      Ende zijn in zijn stede hier gebleven.
705   Dus zijn si boven die enghelen gheset.

KENNISSE Dats waer, diet wel hout onbesmet.
      Mer doen hi hinc met groter smerten
      Aent Cruce, daer gaf hij ons uut Zijnder herten
      Die Seven Sacramenten met seere.
710   Hi en vercoft ons niet, die Heere!
      Hier om dat Sinte Peter lijdt,
      Dat si alle zijn vermaledijt
      Die God copen oft vercopen
      Ende daer af ghelt nemen met hoopen.
715   Si gheven den sondaer quaet exempel.
      Haer kinder lopen inden tempel,
      Ende som sitten si bi wiven

EVERYMAN I will receive God's body with love / and go with humility to the priest. / **FIVE SENSES** Everyman, that is well done. / [685] May God allow you to accomplish this to your salvation! / The priest is above all things: / he teaches us Scripture / and turns humankind from sins. / God has given him more power / [690] than the angels in eternity. / For every priest can without doubt make, / with five words on the altar / during Mass (be sure about this), / God's body, true flesh and blood, / [695] and holds his Creator in his hands. / The priest binds and looses all bonds / in Heaven and on earth. / O noble priest of great worth, / if we kissed your footsteps, you are worthy of it! / [700] Whoever

EVERYMAN   Fayne wolde I receyve that holy body,   *Gladly*
         And mekely to my ghostly father I wyll go.   *spiritual*

FIVE WITS   Everyman, that is the best that ye can do.
731   God wyll you to salvacyon brynge,
         For good Pryesthod excedeth all other thynge.
         To us holy scrypture they do teche
         And converteth man from synne Heven to reche.   *reach*
735   God hath to them more power gyven
         Than to ony angell that is in Heven.   *any*
         With five wordes he may consecrate
         Goddes body in flesshe and bloode to make,
         And handeleth his Maker bytwene his handes.
740   The pryest byndeth and unbyndeth all bandes   *bonds [of sin]*
         Bothe in erth and in Heven.
         Thou mynysters all the Sacrementes seven;   *administer*
         Though we kysse thy fete, thou were worthy,
         Thou arte surgyon that cureth synne deedly.
745   No remedy we fynde under God,
         But all onely Pryesthode.   *Except*
         Everyman, God gave pryest that dygnyté,
         And setteth them in his stede amonge us to be;   *place*
         Thus be they above angelles in degré.

                    [*Exit Everyman to receive last rites*]

KNOWLEDGE   If pryestes be good it is so surely,
751   But whan Jesu henge on the Crosse with great smarte,   *hung; pain*
         There he gave out of his blessyd herte
         The same Sacrament in great tourment.
         He solde them not to us, that Lorde omnipotent;
755   Therefore Saynt Peter the apostle doth saye
         That Jesus curse hathe all they
         Which God theyr Savyour do bye or sell,
         Or they for ony money do take or tell.   *any; count out*
         Synfull pryestes gyveth the synners example bad.
760   Theyr chyldren sytteth by other mennes fires, I have herde,   *heard*
         And some haunteth womens company

---

needs comfort from sins / can find no refuge / but with a priest. / This the Lord has bestowed upon the priest, / and he is present here [in the world] in his place. / [705] Thus he is placed above the angels. / **KNOWLEDGE** That is true, for those who stay unblemished. / When he hung in great pain / on the Cross, he gave us then from his heart / the Seven Sacraments in sorrow. / [710] He did not sell them to us, the Lord! / Therefore St. Peter says / that they are all damned / who buy or sell God / and make heaps of money out of this. / [715] They set a bad example for the sinner. / Their children walk in the temple, / and some of them live with women /

In onsuverheyt van liven.
Dese zijn emmers haers sins onvroet.

VIJF SINNEN Ic hope, of God wil, dat niemant en doet.
721   Daer om laet ons die priesters eeren
        Ende volghen altijt haer leeren.
        Wi zijn haer scapen ende si ons herden,
        Daer wi alle in behoet werden.
725   Laet dit wesen niet meer vermaen.

DUECHT Elckerlijc coemt; hi heeft voldaen.
        Dus laet ons zijn op ons hoede.

ELCKERLIJC Heer God, mi is so wel te moede
        Dat ic van vruechden wene als een kint.
730   Ic hebbe ontfaen mijn Sacrament
        Ende dat Olizel mede. Danc heb diet riet.
        Nu, vrienden, sonder te letten yet,
        Ick danck Gode dat ic u allen vant.
        Slaet aen dit roeyken alle u hant
735   Ende volghet mi haestelic na desen.
        Ick gae vore, daer ic wil wesen.
        Ons Heere God, wil mi gheleyden!

CRACHT Elckerlijc, wi en willen van u niet sceyden,
        Voer ghi ghedaen hebt dese vaert.

VROETSCAP Wi blivens u bi onghespaert,
741   Also wi gheloeft hebben oec langhe.

KENNISSE Och, dits een pelgrimagie seer strange,
        Die Elckerlijc sal moeten gaen.

CRACHT Elckerlijc, siet hoe wi u bi staen:
745   Sterck, vroem, en hebt gheen vaer.

ELCKERLIJC Ay mi, die leden zijn mi so swaer
        Dat si gaen beven voer den gru.

---

in bodily corruption. / They have after all been robbed of their senses. / [720] **FIVE SENSES** I hope, God willing, that none do this. / Let us therefore honor the priests / and always follow their teachings. / We are their sheep and they our shepherds, / by whom we all are protected. / [725] Let's not talk about this anymore. / **VIRTUE** Everyman comes; he has settled up. / Therefore let us all be on guard. / **EVERYMAN** Lord God, I am so happy / that I weep for joy just like a child. / [730] I have received my Sacrament / and the Unction also. Thanks to the one who advised it. / Now, friends, without any further delay, / I thank God that I found all of you. / Place your hands on this little pilgrim's cross /

With unclene lyfe, as lustes of lechery.
These be with synne made blynde.

FIVE WITS   I trust to God no suche may we fynde;
765   Therfore let us Pryesthode honoure
        And folow theyr doctryne for our soules socoure.
        We be ther shepe, and they shepeherdes be
        By whom we all be kepte in suertye.   *security*
        Peas, for yender I se Everyman cume   *Silence; yonder*
770   Which hath made true satysfaccyon.

GOOD DEEDS   Me thynketh it is he indede.

        [Re-enter Everyman]

EVERYMAN   Now Jhesu Cryst be your alder spede.   *helper of all*
        I have receyved the Sacramente for my redempcyon
        And than myne Extreme Unccyon.
775   Blessyd be all they that counceyled me to take it!
        And now, frendes, let us go without longer respyte.   *delay*
        I thanke God that ye have taryed so longe.
        Now set eche of you on this Rodde your honde,   *Rood (Cross)*
        And shortly folwe me.   *expeditiously follow*
780   I go before there I wolde be, God be our guyde.   *go to where*

STRENGTH   Everyman, we wyll not from you go
        Tyll ye have gone this vyage longe.   *journey*

DISCRETION   I, Dyscressyon, wyll byde by you also.   *stand by*

KNOWLEDGE   And though this pylgrimage be never so stronge,   *harsh*
785   I wyll never parte you fro.   *from you*

STRENGTH   Everyman, I wyll be as sure by thee   *steadfast beside you*
        As ever I dyd by Judas Machabé.

        [Procession to the grave]

EVERYMAN   Alas, I am so faynt I may not stande.
        My lymmes under me do folde.

---

[735] and follow me then promptly. / I will lead the way to the place I want to be. / Our Lord God, he will guide me! / **STRENGTH** Everyman, we will not part from you / before you have made this journey. / [740] **PRUDENCE** We will continually stay with you, / as for a long time we have assured you. / **KNOWLEDGE** Oh, this is a very tough pilgrimage, / on which Everyman has to go. / **STRENGTH** Everyman, see how we stand by you: / [745] strong, brave, and have no fear. / **EVERYMAN** Alas, my limbs are so heavy / that they begin to tremble with fear. /

Lieve vrienden, wi en willen niet keeren nu.
Sal ic mijn pelgrimagie betalen,
750   So moet ic hier binnen dalen
In desen put ende werden aerde.

SCHOONHEYT Wat, in desen putte?

ELCKERLIJC   Ja, van desen waerden
Soe moeten wi werden, clein ende groot.

SCHOONHEYT Wat, hier in versmoren?

ELCKERLIJC   Ja, hier in versmoren ende bliven doot
755   Ter werelt, met levende wesen altijt
Voerden oversten Heere.

SCHOONHEYT   Ick schelt u al quijt.
Adieu! Vaert wel! Ic schoer mijn scout; ick gae als de domme.

ELCKERLIJC Wat? Schoonheyt!

SCHOONHEYT   Ic bin al dove; ic en saghe niet omme,
Al mocht mi baten alder werelt schat.

ELCKERLIJC Waer op wil ic mi verlaten?
761   Schoonheyt vliet, oftmense jaechde.
Nochtan te voren, doen ic haer vraechde,
Woude si met mi sterven ende leven.

CRACHT Elckerlijc, ic wil u oec begheven.
765   U spel en behaecht mi niet te deghe.

ELCKERLIJC Cracht, suldi mi oec ontgaen?

CRACHT   Ja, ic wil seker weghe.
Daer mede ghesloten, een voer al.

ELCKERLIJC Lieve Cracht, ontbeyt noch.

CRACHT   Bi Sinte Loy, ick en sal!
769   Waendi dat ic in dien put wil versmoren?

ELCKERLIJC Ende suldi mi dan ontgaen?

Dear friends, let us not turn back now. / If I am to complete my pilgrimage / [750] then I must go down here / into this pit and become earth. / **BEAUTY** What? Into this pit? **EVERYMAN** Yes, into such

790 Frendes, let us not turne agayne to this lande, *return*
Not for all the worldes golde,
For into this cave must I crepe
And turne to erth and there to slepe. *return*

BEAUTY What, into this grave, alas?

EVERYMAN Ye, there shall you consume, more and lesse. *decay*

BEAUTY And what, shulde I smoder here? *smother*

EVERYMAN Ye, be my fayth, and never more appere;
In this worlde lyve no more we shall
799 But in Heven before the hyest Lorde of all.

BEAUTY I crosse out all this. Adew, by Saynte Johnn. *Adieu*
I take my tappe in my lap and am gone. *flax [on distaff]*

EVERYMAN What, Beautye, whether wyll ye? *whither*

BEAUTY Peas, I am defe. I loke not behynde me, *Silence*
Not and thou wolde gyve me all the golde in thy chest. *Not if*

    [*Exit Beauty*]

EVERYMAN Alas, wherto may I truste?
806 Beautye goeth fast awaye and from me.
She promysed with me to lyve and dye.

STRENGTH Everyman, I wyll thee also forsake and denye,
Thy game lyketh me not at all.

EVERYMAN Why, than ye wyll forsake me all.
811 Swete Strength, tary a lytell space.

/ we, both great and small, must turn. / **BEAUTY** What, smother in here? **EVERYMAN** Yes, smother in here and die / [755] to the world, but be alive forever / before the supreme Lord. **BEAUTY** I take back everything. / Adieu! Farewell! I take my leave; I go as the dumb. / **EVERYMAN** What? Beauty! **BEAUTY** I am totally deaf; oh, I do not look back / even if it would gain me all the world's riches. / [760] **EVERYMAN** In what shall I trust? / Beauty flees as if chased away. / Though when I asked her earlier, / she would live and die with me. / **STRENGTH** Everyman, I will also leave you. / [765] Your game does not entirely please me. **EVERYMAN** Strength, will you also flee from me? **STRENGTH** Yes, I will surely go away. / The matter is closed, once and for all. **EVERYMAN** Dear Strength, please wait. **STRENGTH** By St. Eloy I will not! / Do you think that I want to smother in that pit? / [770] **EVERYMAN** Will you leave me then?

CRACHT   Ja ick, tes al verloren,
          Al soudi uwen navel uut crijten.

ELCKERLIJC Suldi aldus u ghelofte quijten?
          Ghi soudt mi bi bliven, so ghi seyt.

CRACHT Ick heb u verre ghenoech gheleyt.
775   Oec sidi oudt ghenoech, ic waen,
          U pelgrimagie alleen te gaen.
          Mi es leet dat icker heden quam.

ELCKERLIJC Ay, lieve Cracht, ic make u gram?

CRACHT Tes al verloren. Rust u hoeft,
780   Ende gaet int doncker huys.

ELCKERLIJC   Dit en had ic u niet gheloeft.
          Wie wil hem verlaten op zijn cracht?
          Si vliet, als mist doet uuter gracht.
          Schoonheit is als wint die vlieghet!
          Ay, getrouwe vrienden, dat ghi dus lieget,
785   Ghi seydet mi toe schoon ter kore.

VROETSCAP Elckerlijc, ic wil oeck gaen dore
          Ende nemen uutstel van desen.
          Waendi dat wi hier in willen wesen?
789   Hoet u van dien, ic wils mi wachten.

ELCKERLIJC   O Vroetscap, Vroetscap!

VROETSCAP   Ick en wil niet mede.
          Tes verloren ghevroetscapt, claer.

ELCKERLIJC Lieve Vroescap, coemt doch soe nae,
          Dat ghi hier binnen den gront aensiet.
          Ick bidts u oetmoedelijc.

VROETSCAP   Bi Sinte Loy, ick en doe des niet!
795   Mi rouwet dat icker ye quam so bi.

STRENGTH Yes, it is all in vain, / though you may cry yourself into a hernia. / **EVERYMAN** Will you thus redeem your promise? / You said you would stay with me. / **STRENGTH** I have guided you far enough. / [775] Then too, you are old enough, I think, / to go on your pilgrimage alone. / I regret now that I came here. / **EVERYMAN** Alas, dear Strength, am I angering you? / **STRENGTH** It is all in vain. Rest your head, / [780] and go into that dark house. **EVERYMAN** I had never thought this of you. / Who will trust in his Strength? / It flees like mist from the ditch. / Beauty is like a wind that flees! / Alas, trusty friends, that you lie so, / [785] after making promises to me. **PRUDENCE** Everyman, I also

STRENGTH	Nay, syr, by the Rode of Grace,	*Rood (Cross)*
	I wyll hye me from thee fast	
814	Though thou wepe tyll thy harte brast.	*until; bursts*

EVERYMAN	Ye wolde ever byde by me, ye sayd.	*abide*

STRENGTH	Ye, I have you ferre ynought convayed.	*far; accompanied*
	Ye be olde ynough, I understande,	
	Your pylgrymage to take on hande.	*in hand*
	I repente me that I hether came.	

EVERYMAN	Strength, you to dysplease I am to blame.	
821	Wyll you breke promyse that is dette?	*an obligation*

STRENGTH	In faith, I care not.	
	Thou arte but a foole to complayne.	
	You spende your speche and waste your brayne.	*expend*
825	Go, thryst thee into the grounde.	*thrust yourself*

        [Exit Strength]

EVERYMAN	I had wende surer I shulde you have founde.	*had thought more loyal*
	He that trusteth in his Strength,	
	She hym deceyveth at the length.	
	Bothe Strength and Beautye forsaketh me,	
830	Yet they promysed me fayre and lovyngly.	

DISCRETION	Everyman, I wyll after Strength be gone.	
	As for me, I wyll leve you alone.	

EVERYMAN	Why, Descressyon, wyll ye forsake me?	

DISCRETION	Ye, in fayth, I wyll go from thee,	
835	For whan Strength goeth before,	
	I folow after evermore.	

EVERYMAN	Yet I pray thee for the love of the Trynytye,	
	Loke in my grave ones pyteously.	*once with pity*

DISCRETION	Nay, so nye I wyll not cume.	*near*
840	Farewell, everychone.	*everyone*

---

will go away / and wish to put this off. / Do you think that we want to go in here? / Don't think of it, I know better. / [790] **EVERYMAN** O Prudence, Prudence! **PRUDENCE** I will not go with you. / It is clearly imprudent. / **EVERYMAN** Dear Prudence, come at least closer, / so that you can see the bottom of the earth in here. / I humbly beg this of you. **PRUDENCE** By St. Eloy, I will not do this! / [795] I regret that I ever came so close. /

Elckerlijc Och, al mist, dat God niet en si.
　　　　Schoonheyt, Cracht, ende Vroescap groot,
　　　　Het vliet van Elckerlijc, als coemt de Doot.
799　　Arm mensche, waer sal ic nu op lenen?

Vijf Sinnen Elckerlijc, ic wil oec henen
　　　　Ende volghen den anderen die u ontwerven.

Elckerlijc　　　　　　Och, lieve Vijf Sinnen!

Vijf Sinnen Ick en wil daer niet aen winnen.
　　　　Dat ghi veel roept, ten mach nyet baten.

Elckerlijc Och, suldi mi alle gader laten?

Duecht Neen wi, Elckerlijc. Zijt ghestelt.

Elckerlijc Ay mi, mijn Vijf Sinnen!

Vijf Sinnen　　　　　Roept al dat ghi wilt.
807　　Ghi en sult ni niet meer van voor bekijken.

Elckerlijc Lieve Duecht, blijft ghi bi mi?

Duecht　　　　　　Ick en sal u nemmermeer beswijken,
　　　　Om leven, om sterven, of om gheen torment.

Elckerlijc Hier zijn ghetrouwe vrienden bekent.
811　　Alle die mi ontgaen ghemeene,
　　　　Die mindic meer dan mijn Duecht alleene.
　　　　Kennisse, suldi mi oec begheven?

Kennisse Ja ic, Elckerlijc, als ghi eyndet u leven,
815　　Mer seker niet eer, om gheen dangier.

Elckerlijc Danck hebt, Kennisse.

Kennisse　　　　　　Ick en scheyde niet van hier
　　　　Voer dat ghi zijt daer ghi behoort.

Elckerlijc Mi dunckt, wacharmen, wij moeten voert,
　　　　Rekeninghe doen ende ghelden mijn scult.

Everyman Oh, everything that is not God will fail. / Beauty, Strength, great Prudence, / they fly from Everyman when Death approaches. / Poor mankind, on whom shall I rely now? / [800] **Five Senses** Everyman, I will also leave / and follow the others who turn their backs on you. **Everyman** Oh, dear Five Senses! / **Five Senses** I will not gain anything from this; / it is no use to cry so much. / **Everyman** Oh, are you all going to leave me? / [805] **Virtue** No, Everyman. Rest assured. / **Everyman** Alas,

[*Exit Discretion*]

EVERYMAN   O, all thynge fayleth save God alone,
　　　　　Beautye, Strength, and Descressyon,
　　　　　For whan Deth bloweth his blaste   *[trumpet] blast*
　　　　　They all renne from me full fast.   *run*

FIVE WITS   Everyman, of thee now my leve I take;
846　　　I wyll folow the other, for here I thee forsake.   *others*

EVERYMAN   Alas, than, may I wayle and wepe,
　　　　　For I toke you for my best frende.

FIVE WITS   I wyll no lenger thee kepe.
850　　　Now farwell, and there an ende.

　　　　　[*Exit Five Wits*]

EVERYMAN   O Jesu, helpe, all hath forsaken me.

GOOD DEEDS   Nay, Everyman, I wyll byde wyth thee.   *abide*
　　　　　I wyll not forsake thee indede;
　　　　　Thou shalte fynde me a good frende at nede.

EVERYMAN   Gramercy, Good Dedes, now may I true frendes se.
856　　　They have forsaken me everychone.   *everyone*
　　　　　I loved them better then my Good Dedes alone.
　　　　　Knowlege, wyll ye forsake me also?

KNOWLEDGE   Ye, Everyman, whan ye to deth do go,
860　　　But not yet, for no maner of daungere.

EVERYMAN   Gramercy, Knowlege, with all my herte.

KNOWLEDGE   Naye, yet I wyll not from hens departe   *hence*
　　　　　Tyll I se where ye shall become.   *what will become of you*

EVERYMAN   Me thynketh, alas, that I must be gone
865　　　To make my rekenynge and my dettes paye,   *debts*

---

my Five Senses! **FIVE SENSES** Cry all that you want. / You will not see my face again. / **EVERYMAN** Dear Virtue, will you stay with me? **VIRTUE** I will never leave you in the lurch, / for life, death, or any torment. / [810] **EVERYMAN** You are able to know your true friends here. / Those who leave me altogether, / I loved them more than my Virtue alone. / Knowledge, will you also leave me? / **KNOWLEDGE** Yes, Everyman, when you end your life, / [815] but definitely not before, no danger of that. / **EVERYMAN** Thank you, Knowledge. **KNOWLEDGE** I will not depart from here / before you are where you belong. / **EVERYMAN** Alas, I think we must go on, / to give reckoning and pay my debt. /

820   Want mijn tijt is schier vervult.
        Neemter exempel aen, diet hoort ende siet.
        Ende merct hoet nu al van mi vliet:
        Sonder mijn Duecht wil met mi varen.

DUECHT   Alle aertsche dinghen zijn al niet.

ELCKERLIJC   Duecht, merct hoet nu al van mi vliet.

DUECHT   Schoonheyt, Cracht, Vroescap, dat hem liet,
827   Tgheselscap, die Vrienden ende Magen waren.

ELCKERLIJC   Nu merct hoet nu al van mi vliet,
        Sonder mijn Duecht, die wil mit mi varen.
830   Ghenade, Coninck der enghelen scharen,
        Ghenade, Moeder Gods, staet mi bi.

DUECHT   Ic sal mi puer voer Gode verclaren.

ELCKERLIJC   Ghenade, Coninc der enghelen scharen!

DUECHT   Cort ons die pine, sonder verswaren,
835   Maect ons deynde los ende vri.

ELCKERLIJC   Ghenade, Coninck der enghelen scharen,
        Ghenade, Moeder Gods, staet mi bi.
        In uwen handen, Vader, hoe dat si,
        Beveel ic u minen gheest in vreden.
840   Ick vare metter Duecht.

KENNISSE   Hi heeft leden
        Dat wij alle moeten gelden.
        Die Duecht sal nu haer selven melden
        Voer hem diet al ordelen sal.
        Mi dunct ic hore der enghelen gheschal
845   Hier boven; den Hemel is seker ontdaen,
        Daer Elckerlijc binnen sal zijn ontfaen.

---

[820] My time is almost up. / Whoever hears and sees this: take example from it. / And see how all flee from me; / my Virtue only will go with me. / **VIRTUE** All earthly things are nothing at all. / [825] **EVERYMAN** But see, Virtue, how all flee from me now. / **VIRTUE** Beauty, Strength, Prudence, who deserted him, / Fellowship, who were Friends and Kinsmen. / **EVERYMAN** Now see how all flee from me, / except my Virtue, who will go with me. / [830] Mercy, King of the angelic host, / Mercy, Mother of God, stand by me. / **VIRTUE** I will appear unblemished before God. / **EVERYMAN** Mercy, King of

For I se my tyme is nye spente awaye.   *is nearly expired*
Take example all ye that this do here or se   *hear or see*
How they that I loved best do forsake me
Excepte my Good Dedes that bydeth truly.

Good Deeds All erthly thynge is but vanyté;
871   Beauté, Strength, and Discrecyon do man forsake,
           Folysshe frendes and kynnesmen that fayre spake,
           All fleeth save Good Dedes, and that am I.

Everyman Have mercy on me, God moost myghty,
875   And stande by me thou moder and mayde, holy Mary.   *mother*

Good Deeds Fere not, I wyll speke for thee.

Everyman Here I crye God mercy.

Good Deeds Shorte oure ende and mynysshe our payne,   *shorten; lessen*
           Let us go and never come agayne.

Everyman Into thy handes, Lord, my soule I commende,
881   Receyve it, Lorde, that it be nat lost.   *not*
           As thou me boughtest so me defende,
           And save me from the fendes boost   *fiend's boast*
           That I may appere with that blessed hoost
885   That shall be saved at the Dome.   *Last Judgment*
           In manus tuas, of myghtes moost   *Into your hands*
           Forever, *commendo spiritum meum*.   *I commend my soul*

           [*Everyman and Good Deeds enter the grave*]

Knowledge Now hath he suffred that we all shall endure.   *that which*
           The Good Dedes shall make all sure;
890   Now hathe he made endynge.
           Me thynketh that I here angelles synge   *hear*
           And make great joye and melodye
           Where Everymannes soule shall receyved be.

---

the angelic host! / **Virtue** Shorten the pain for us, do not let it worsen, / [835] make the end for us light and free. / **Everyman** Mercy, King of the angelic host, / Mercy, Mother of God, stand by me. / Into thy hands, Father, however it may be, / I commend to you my spirit in peace. / [840] I go with Virtue. **Knowledge** He has undergone / what we all have to pay. / Virtue will now herself testify / before him who shall judge everything. / I think I hear the sound of angels / [845] here above; certainly, Heaven is opened, / wherein Everyman will be taken in. /

Die Ynghel seyt:

Coemt uutvercoren bruyt,
Hier boven, ende hoort dat suete gheluyt
Der engelen mits uwe goede Virtuyt.
850   Die siele neem ick den lichaem uut:
Haer rekeninghe is puer ende reyne.
Nu voer icse in des Hemels pleyne,
Daer wi alle moeten ghemeene
In comen, groot ende cleene.
        Amen.

DIE NAEPROLOGHE

855   Neemt in dancke, cleyn ende groot,
Ende siet hoe Elckerlijc coemt ter Doot.
Gheselscap, Vrienden, ende Goet
Gaet Elckerlijc af; zijt des vroet.
Scoonheyt, Cracht, Vroescap, ende Vijf Sinnen,
860   Tes al verganclijc, zijt des te binnen.
Sonder die Duecht volcht voer al.
Mer als die Duecht is so smal
Dat si niet mede en mach oft en kan,
Arm Elckerlijc, hoe vaerdi dan
865   Ter rekeninghen voer onsen Heere?
Dan gadi van wee, van seere,
Want na die Doot eerst quaet te verhalen;
Daer en baet voerspraec noch tale.
Ay, Elckerlijc, hoe moechdi wesen
870   Hovaerdich, nidich!
                        Seer uut ghelesen,
Merct desen spieghel, hebten voer oghen
Ende wilt u van hovardien poghen
Ende oec van allen sonden met.
Nu laet ons bidden onghelet
875   Dat dit elck mensche moet vesten
Dat wi voer Gode suver comen ten lesten.
Des gonne ons die hemelsche Vader.
"Amen" segghet alle gader.
        God heb lof!

The Angel says: / Come chosen bride, / here above, and hear that sweet sound / of the angels because of your good Virtue. / [850] I take the soul out of the body: / her reckoning is pure and clean. / Now I take her onto the plain of Heaven, / where all together we may / enter, great and small. / Amen. / **THE EPILOGUE** / [855] Accept this, small and great, / and see how Everyman comes to his Death. / Fellowship, Friends, and Goods / desert Everyman; be sure about this. / Beauty, Strength, Prudence, and Five Senses, / [860] it is all fleeting, bear this in mind. / Only Virtue follows before all others. / But

ANGEL	Cume, excellent electe spouse to Jesu.	*chosen bride*
895	Here above thou shall go	
	Bycause of thy synguler vertue.	
	Now thy soule is taken thy body fro	*from the body*
	Thy rekenynge is crystall clere.	
	Now shalt thou into the hevenly spere	*sphere*
900	Unto the whiche all ye shall cume	
	That lyveth well before the Day of Dome.	*Doom*

[The angel takes Everyman's soul to Heaven]

[Enter Doctor]

DOCTOR	This memoryall men may have in mynde.	*mnemonic aid*
	Ye herers take it of worth olde and yonge	*hearers; value it greatly*
	And forsake Pryde, for he deceyveth you in the ende,	
905	And remembre Beautye, Fyve Wyttes, Strength, and Discression.	
	They all at the last do Everyman forsake,	
	Save his Good Dedes, there dothe he take.	
	But beware, for and they be small	*for [even] if*
	Before God, he hath no helpe at all.	
910	None excuse may be there for Everyman.	
	Alas, how shall he do than?	*what shall; then*
	For after deth amendes may no man make,	
	For than Mercy and Petye doeth hym forsake	*Pity*
	If his rekenynge be not clere whan he do cume.	
915	God wyll saye, "*Ite maledicti in ignem eternum.*"	*Go, wicked ones, into the eternal fire*
	And he that hath his accounte hole and sounde	
	Hye in Heven he shall be crounde,	
	Unto the whiche place God brynge us all thether	
	That we may lyve, body and soule togyther.	
920	Therto helpe, the Trynytye,	
	Say ye for saynte charytye,	
	Amen.	

when Virtue is so weak / that she may or cannot come along, / poor Everyman, how then will you go / [865] to the reckoning before the Lord? / Then you will perish of woe, of pain, / for after Death it is difficult to reform; / no intercession or pleading will help you then. / Ah, Everyman, how are you able to be / [870] proud, envious! Very honorable audience, / mark this mirror, hold it before your eyes / and avoid pride / and all other sins as well. / Now let us pray at once / [875] that this may be imprinted into everyone's heart / in order that we come pure before God in the end. / May the heavenly Father grant us this. / Say "Amen" all together. / God be praised!

❧ Explanatory Notes to *Everyman*

Abbreviations: **Cawley**: *Everyman*, ed. Cawley (rpt. 1977); **Dent**: Dent, *Proverbial Language in English Drama exclusive of Shakespeare, 1495–1616*; **Tilley**: Tilley, *Dictionary of the Proverbs in England*; **Whiting**: Whiting, *Proverbs, Sentences and Proverbial Phrases from English Writings*.

1–21   The Messenger's speech is not present in the extant text of *Elckerlijc*, and may be the work of the translator.

6   *How transytory we be all daye*. Messenger calls attention to the transitory nature of human life. As Cooper and Wortham note in their edition of *Everyman* (p. 2), this motif appears in the Dance of Death tradition, which is invoked in the title-page woodcut used for the editions of the play printed by John Skot. See Introduction, pp. 6–7.

8   *more gracyous*. More filled with grace (i.e., God's saving grace).

10–11   *in the begynnynge . . . endynge*. Proverbial; see Dent, F386. Compare *Worlde and the Chylde*, ed. Davidson and Happé, lines 484–85, and Tilley, E128; Whiting, E84. Cawley further suggests a source in Ecclesiasticus 7:36.

16–17   *Jolyté . . . Pleasure*. A mistake. These two allegorical characters do not appear in the play.

18   *vade from thee as floure in Maye*. Proverbial. As Death explains in the Lansdowne manuscript version of Lydgate's *Dance of Death*, life "may be likned in all thyng / Unto a Flour . . . / Which with a Froste bigynneth riht sone to fade" (lines 236–38).

20   *rekenynge*. See Introduction, p. 8n42.

23   *unkynde*. Not only unappreciative or even blasphemous in speech and act but also unnatural. An actor playing the role of God would have been positioned at a higher level representing Heaven, as demonstrably is the case in some of the mystery plays. The figure of God is necessarily Christ, who suffered for humankind, as lines 29–33 demonstrate. The iconographic tradition would suggest that he should show his wounds at the appropriate points in his speech.

29   *My lawe*. Replacing the Old Law of the Old Testament, this is the law of mercy and the offer of salvation made available by Christ's act of suffering and sacrificial death on the Cross, when he was crowned with thorns and hung between two thieves.

33   *I heled theyr fete*. A reference to the washing of the disciples' feet (John 13:4–12).

36–37   *Seven Deedly Synnes . . . / As Pryde, Covetyse, Wrathe, and Lechery.* Gluttony, Sloth, and Envy are omitted. Cawley notes (p. 29) that these "are sufficient to represent the World, the Flesh, and the Devil," which were known as the Three Enemies of Man. *Elckerlijc* likewise presents an incomplete list, including only Pride, Avarice, and Envy — sins that may be regarded as most appropriately mentioned in the context of the Dutch mercantile culture.

41   *theyr.* There is a shift here to plural, indicating that Everyman means "every man" or, in preferred modern terms, "every person," all humans.

50   *one wolde by envy another up ete.* For a comparison with *King Lear* 4.2.46–50, see Salter, "*Lear* and the Morality Tradition"; Cawley suggests the influence of Galatians 5:15: "But if you bite and devour one another; take heed you be not consumed one of another."

51   *Charytye.* See Introduction, p. 8.

53   *mansyon.* John 14:2 promises that Heaven will contain "many mansions."

54   *electe.* Chosen by God's divine will, but here not implying predestination since good works are required for salvation. See Ryan, "Doctrine and Dramatic Structure," pp. 723–25.

57   *theyr beynge that I them have lente.* Humans are not autonomous creatures, but owe their being to God. Kolve, "*Everyman* and the Parable of the Talents," convincingly suggests that a major influence on the play is the parable of the talents, in which the servants are required to make a reckoning to their master upon his return from a distant land (Matthew 25:14–30).

63   *messengere.* Death is God's agent who brings news of one's inevitable end, an end common to all men and women, as in the Dance of Death tradition. At line 330, the protagonist calls Death the "hye Kinges chefe offycere." Owst, *Literature and Pulpit*, p. 532, calls attention to a comment in a sermon collection (Cambridge, Caius College MS 334) by John Waldeby of the Augustinian friary at York concerning the point in life "when Death, who is God's Bailiff, shall come to arrest" a man or woman. For another instance in drama in which Death is "Goddys masangere," see the death of Herod sequence in the N-Town plays (20.168–284), but in that case Death's role is different since he is an avenger to execute justice on a wicked monarch.

68   *pylgrymage.* The notion of life as a pilgrimage culminating in death was a commonplace and needs to be seen in the context of pilgrimage practice of the time, when one had to leave one's comfortable life and possessions behind as one set out from the city gates (in the case of guild members, accompanied only that far by one's fellow guildsmen) to travel, often walking, to holy sites of worship and veneration, many of them at great distances away. Scholars sometimes speak of pilgrims' experiences as liminal or liminoid (see Turner, "Liminal to Liminoid"), a term applicable to Everyman in this play.

76   *stryke with my darte.* Death's dart or spear is a commonplace of iconography, as in the deathbed scene in the famous Corporal Acts of Mercy window at All

Saints, North Street, York. Death's weaponry is surveyed by Oosterwijk ("Lessons in 'Hopping'"), who cites the brass of John Rudyng at Biggleswade, Bedfordshire, which not only shows Death armed with several spears but also includes his description of himself, which she translates as follows: "I carry grim weapons, I harrass the world hard with the bite of violent death" (ibid., pp. 262–63, figs. 4–5). Though Death gives no warning, he may carry a bell that does. In MS Douce 322, fol. 19v, Death holds both a spear and a bell, the latter ringing out "dethe, deye, deye" all across the image (Pächt and Alexander, *Illuminated Manuscripts*, no. 1097, pl. 102). As noted in the Introduction to the present edition, the title page of the Vorsterman text of *Elckerlijc* shows Death striking the protagonist with a spear. In *Everyman*, lines 178–79, Death threatens to "smyte" without warning and "to the harte." A short lyric in a fourteenth-century commonplace book (National Library of Scotland, Advocates' MS 18.7.21, fol. 87) concludes: "Deth is an Hardy Huntere" (Wilson, *Descriptive Index*, p. 23). See also Introduction, above, pp. 6–7.

78   *almes dedes.* Good works, essential for salvation.

81   *Full lytell he thynketh on my cummynge.* Death is also utterly unexpected in the *Dance of Death* by Lydgate. It is proverbial that death is certain, the time of death uncertain. A Latin form of this proverb is included in John of Grimestone's commonplace book (fol. 87v); quoted by Wilson, *Descriptive Index*, p. 25. See also Tilley, *Elizabethan Proverb Lore*, p. 82.

95   *in the hevenly spere.* Since *Elckerlijc* has "in sijn rijck" ("in his kingdom"), this is a sign that the translator thought more specifically of an actor playing God stationed at a higher level that represents the region in medieval cosmology which is identified as the sphere encircling all the lower spheres of the moon, the sun, the planets, and the stars.

113   *gyve.* The original reading was apparently "gyve now," to rhyme with "thou" (Kölbing, "Kleine Beiträge zur Erklärung," as cited by Cawley, p. 31).

114   *I knowe thee not.* In their edition Cooper and Wortham compare Everyman's failure to recognize Death with the Dance of Death "whereby Death is not recognized by the other participants of the dance until he singles them out" (p. 14).

116   *rest.* Compare *Hamlet* 5.2.336–37: "As this fell sergeant, Death, / Is strict in his arrest."

126   *pope, emperoure, kynge, duke, ne prynces.* The order is reminiscent of the "descending order of importance" of the characters in the Dance of Death (Cawley, p. 31).

127   *and I wolde receyve geftes.* It is proverbial that Death takes no bribes. Tilley, D149; Dent, D149.

132   *Deth geveth no warnynge.* Proverbial. See explanatory note to line 81, above.

142   *prove thy frendes yf thou can.* In the tradition of friendship going back to antiquity, testing of one's friends was considered to be "the first law of friendship" (Conley, "Doctrine of Friendship in *Everyman*," p. 375). In the form of the story recorded in the *Gesta Romanorum*, the young man, a knight, sets out first to find and then

to test friends at the behest of his father, a Roman emperor (*Early English Versions of the Gesta Romanorum*, ed. Herrtage, pp. 127–31). *Everyman* keeps to the motif of testing more clearly than *Elckerlijc*.

143   *the tyde abydeth no man.* Proverbial; see Whiting, T318; Dent, T323.

145   *For Adams synne must dye of nature.* See Genesis 3:19. In line 585, below, Adam is said to have "forfeyted" life "by his dysobedyens"; hence all humans, who inherit Adam's lapsarian state, require redemption from their natural condition.

148   *saynt charyté.* Holy charity. Not a saint, but the invocation of charitable acts, by which salvation is made possible for the individual Christian. See Introduction, p. 8.

149   *Sholde I not come agayne shortly?* To this question, Death (in lines 150–52) will affirm the finality of dying and thus will deny metempsychosis or the return of the soul to earthly life within another body.

153   *in hye sete celestyall.* Another sign that God is imagined by the writer to be positioned on high, in this case on a throne, as in the Towneley Creation pageant where such a seat is indicated.

155   *vale terestyall.* As God exists on a (heavenly) height (see line 153), so also humans dwell in an earthly valley.

164   *it was but lend thee.* Referring to both life and possessions, mentioned in lines 161–62. Because of death, ownership can only be temporary. In the lines which follow, Death will continue to explain how property will be passed on to others, who in turn will also eventually need to surrender it. Absolute control of one's life and possessions is an illusion. For an example in an earlier morality play, see *Castle of Perseverance*, lines 2969–3007, and Fletcher, "Coveytyse Copbord." Anderson, *Drama and Imagery*, p. 77, calls attention to a misericord in a Dance of Death series at St. George's Chapel, Windsor, in which the rich man, situated among his chests of treasure and other signs of wealth, is approached by Death. There was a shift to concern about covetousness that corresponded with the increased wealth of the late Middle Ages; see Little, "Pride Goes before Avarice."

168   *wyttes fyve.* Here the reference is merely to the five senses and not to the personification, Five Wits, who will later appear in the play at line 669.

171   *whether shall I flee.* Compare Vulgate Psalm 138:7.

178   *to the harte sodenly I shall smyte.* The Dutch had specified "int crijt" ("in the ring"), which would refer to a duel or tournament; in either case, a circle or other marked-out space for a competition.

182–83   *"This is the day . . . awaye."* Proverbial. The day of death, but the words also may echo the opening words (in Latin) of the gradual for Easter: "Haec dies." It is a time of terror for Everyman, but it is also, even for one who has been neglectful of his spiritual life, a time that ultimately will translate into hope and then joy, which have been made possible by the Resurrection of Christ.

199   *affyaunce*. As Cooper and Wortham note in their edition, this word's meaning also extends to a legal sense, "solemn promise or sworn agreement" (p. 18).

215   *well spoken and lovyngly*. Corresponding to "Ghi segt wel, boven screve" ("You speak well, certainly") in *Elckerlijc*, a line omitted in van Elslander, and numbered 205 — with the next line numbered 205a — in our edition to maintain consistent line numbering for convenient reference to his edition. This line occurs not only in the Vorsterman edition but also in the Govaert Bac edition of c. 1501 and Brussels, Bibliothèque royale MS. IV–592. It is lacking only in the Snellaert edition of 1496.

217   *I have pytye . . . destresse*. The corresponding line in Dutch literally reads "you are so full of sadness, one could cut it out of you."

218   *ye shall revenged be*. Fellowship is prone to wrath, of which being quick to revenge is a characteristic. However, as demonstrated subsequently, he is bluffing and hence proves himself to be both a braggart and a coward. See also lines 281–82.

222   *set not a straw*. Proverbial; see Whiting, S813; Dent, S917.

229   *a good frende at nede*. An echo of the proverb "A friend in need is a friend indeed"; see Tilley, F693; Whiting, F634.

245   *Adonay*. God (Hebrew), as a judge.

248   *Promyse is dutye*. Proverbial; compare Dent, P603; and Tilley, P603: "Promise is debt."

265   *by God that all hath bought*. Through his atonement, Christ "bought" those who will be saved from Satan, whose rights to these souls were thus abrogated.

267   *For no man . . . lyvynge*. The literal translation of the corresponding line in the Dutch text is "for all creatures that God allows to live."

272–73   *ete and drynke . . . haunte to women*. Implying Gluttony and Lechery, two of the Seven Deadly Sins that were associated with Fellowship. In the speech of God at the beginning of the play, Gluttony was not mentioned; see note to lines 36–37, above.

288   *By Saynt Johnn*. An appropriate oath, since St. John the Baptist has associations with the revelry of Midsummer, which occurred on the vigil of this saint's nativity (St. John's Eve, June 23).

292   *gyve me a new gowne*. Lester, citing the *Paston Letters*, notes that "payments were sometimes made in this way, and an old gown was sometimes given as a gratuity" (*Everyman*, ed. Lester, p. 75). But a new gown would be an expensive gift. The reference to a gown is absent in *Elckerlijc*.

302   *partynge is mournynge*. Proverbial; see Tilley, P82. Cawley cites *Romeo and Juliet* 2.2.184: "Parting is such sweet sorrow."

309–10   "*In prosperyté . . . unkynde.*" Proverbial. Compare Ecclesiasticus 6:10: "And there is a friend, a companion at the table, and he will not abide in the day of distress." See also Whiting, F659; Dent, T301.

316   *For kynde wyll crepe where it may not go.* Proverbial; Whiting, K34; Dent, K49. Kin-
       ship relations may be called on covertly if not openly. Cawley notes the Towneley
       Secunda Pastorum: "I trow kynde will crepe / Where it may not go" (*Towneley
       Plays*, ed. Stevens and Cawley, 13.853–54). *Elckerlijc* has the Dutch proverb cor-
       responding to the modern "Blood is thicker than water."

318   *frendes and kynnesmen.* The Dutch has "Maghe," kin on his mother's side, and
       "Neve," kin on his father's side; these have been identified in our translation of
       Elckerlijc for convenience as Kinsman and Cousin.

334   *great enemy that hath me in wayte.* The Devil, whose purpose is to capture Every-
       man's soul at the moment of death. The iconography occurs in treatises on
       dying in which a devil waits in proximity to the deathbed. The wicked will be
       snatched away by him, while those who merit salvation will be saved from his
       clutches by their guardian angels.

346   *I had lever fast breed and water.* Probably proverbial; see Dent, B611.11.

348   *Alas that ever I was borne.* A sign of despair that is warned against in the *ars
       moriendi* texts, of which *The Art and Crafte to Knowe Well to Dye* (1490) was the first
       English edition. For a convenient summary, see Beaty, *Craft of Dying*, pp. 12–13.
       The phrasing here is proverbial; see Dent, B140.1.

353   *by Saynt Anne.* St. Anne, the Virgin Mary's mother, was a popular saint, suitable
       here for Kindred's oath, though her name also provides a convenient rhyme.

379   *fayre wordes maketh fooles fayne.* Proverbial; see Dent, W794. Cawley (p. 33) cites
       Early English Miscellanies, ed. Halliwell: "Fayre promese ofte maketh foollis fayne."

411   *to clene and puryfye.* Theologically this would only be possible through the action
       of baptism, penance, and absolution, which are activated through God's sancti-
       fying grace. See line 536, below, in which Everyman is urged by Knowledge to
       go to Confession, who is described as a "clensynge ryvere" — and in line 545
       also as a "gloryous fountayne that all unclennes doth clarify."

413   *"money maketh all ryght that is wronge."* Proverbial; see Whiting, M630; Dent,
       M1072. A verse in John of Grimestone's commonplace book begins "Pecunia
       maket wrong riht" (fol. 14; quoted by Owst, *Literature and Pulpit*, p. 317).

414   *I synge another songe.* Proverbial; see Whiting S478 and Dent, S637.

419   *Thy rekenynge I have made blotted and blynde.* A sign of Goods' envy (one of the
       Seven Deadly Sins), which would lead Everyman to his damnation, as Cooper
       and Wortham note in their edition (p. 28). Everyman, in turn, is here identified
       with Covetousness, another of the Deadly Sins (cited in line 37, above), for his
       love of Goods.

423   *ferefull answere.* The answer (giving an accounting) that Everyman must give to
       God at the Last Judgment.

431   *yf thou had me loved moderately.* If you had valued riches as a means rather than
       an end.

437   *wenest thou that I am thyne?* See explanatory note on line 164, above.

458   *I gave thee that whiche shulde be the Lordes above.* Inordinate love of Goods is
        idolatry. Cawley, p. 33, further cites Chaucer's Parson's Tale: "Soothly, whan
        man loveth any creature moore than Jhesu Crist oure Creatour, thanne is it
        deedly synne" (*CT* X[I]357). See St. Augustine, *On Christian Doctrine* 3.10.16 for
        an authoritative definition of the proposition.

481   *Good Dede.* The Dutch text specifies "Duecht." This term appears in our trans-
        lation as Virtue but implies very much the same thing as Good Deeds.

486   *colde in the grounde.* Not lying ill in bed, paralyzed, as in *Elckerlijc*; see note to line
        487, below, for the more theologically astute reference in *Everyman* to being in
        bondage, with the physical depiction symbolizing spiritual condition.

487   *synnes have me so sore bounde.* Good Deeds' fetters represent the bonds of sin from
        which release is possible, according to Catholic theology, only through loosing
        by means of the power of the keys granted to St. Peter and thereafter to the
        Church; see Matthew 16:19. The crisis for Everyman is that he cannot achieve
        salvation unless he is loosed from the weight of his sins and his Good Deeds
        released from her bondage to assist him to his salvation, for without her he is
        lost. See lines 509–10 below, in which Everyman begs Good Deeds' help, "Or els
        I am forever damned indede." Good deeds are also proclaimed as a requirement
        for salvation in *Elckerlijc*.

494   *of Jerusalem Kynge.* The heavenly Jerusalem, of which Christ is King.

501   *Yf ye had perfytely chered me.* Conley, "'If ye had parfytely chered me,'" notes a
        range of meanings for *cheren* and argues that Everyman should have extended
        to Good Deeds, now in the position of a person needing charity, those acts of
        kindness which would have included welcoming her into his house, giving her
        to drink and eat, and allowing her to warm herself at his fire — that is, three of
        the acts specified in Matthew 25 which later were codified as Corporal Acts of
        Mercy.

520   *Knowlege.* In the moral and spiritual sense of the word as well as an indication
        of knowledge of Christian doctrine and practice. This therefore implies self-
        knowledge in the sense of recognition of one's faults and sins.

527   *she.* Knowledge, which will lead Everyman to the House of Salvation where his
        "smarte" or source of pain will be healed; sin is conceived as an illness. The
        emendation to "she" is based on the identification of Knowledge as Good Deeds'
        sister (line 519), as suggested by Cooper and Wortham. Her gender is consistent
        with *Elckerlijc*.

540   *House of Salvacyon.* Meant to be understood as a specific location, probably a
        booth set at the back of the stage as depicted in Flemish illustrations of the time;
        see Hummelen, "Drama of the Dutch Rhetoricians," p. 235. The House of Sal-
        vation of course represents the Church, the structure within which salvation is
        possible.

543   *Confessyon.* Below cited as Shrift, the "mother of Salvacyon" (line 552), though,
        differing from *Elckerlijc*, Confession is identified by masculine pronouns. Auricu-

lar confession is the second part of the Sacrament of Penance, following Contrition.

545   *gloryous fountayne*. See explanatory note to line 411. For the fountain as a sign of saving grace made effective through the Eucharist, see Davidson, "Repentance and the Fountain." Cawley cites Zacharias 13:1: "In that day there shall be a fountain open to the house of David, and to the inhabitants of Jerusalem: for the washing of the sinner, and of the unclean woman." In a poem in Arundel MS 286, Jesus' "woundes so wide / ben welles of life" from which people are urged "to drinke" in order "to fle fro the fendes of helle" (Browne, *Religious Lyrics of the Fifteenth Century*, p. 149). Cunningham cites an accession prayer, included in the Burntisland edition of the Sarum missal, which not only mentions the medicinal and cleansing benefits (spiritually speaking) of coming to the fountain of mercy but also outlines "in small the journey which Everyman makes" ("Comedic and Liturgical Restoration," pp. 164–65). *Everyman* corrects the Dutch text as it has come down to us and which specifies "Bloome" ("flower").

549   *full contrycyon*. Sorrow for one's sins; the second part of the Sacrament of Penance, designated by Confession as a jewel (line 557).

561   *scurge*. The scourge of penance, in this case made of rope, since it is described as having knots at line 576. Though the type of penitential scourge varies, this is conventional iconography; see Nichols, *Seeable Signs*, pp. 235–38. Anderson, *Drama and Imagery*, p. 80, cites a misericord at New College, Oxford, which has Confession set off against, on the other side, a figure scourging himself. With the scourge one would have been expected to replicate the suffering of Christ at his scourging (see line 563) and thereby to identify with his Passion. (An excellent depiction of knotted rope scourges may be found in a Scourging in the Hildburgh Collection in the Victoria and Albert Museum; see Cheetham, *English Medieval Alabasters*, no. 163.) However, while Jesus was innocent, Everyman has clearly been guilty, as he indicates when he turns the scourge on himself at lines 611–18, and the self-punishment is a way of expiation for him. For an explicit connection between satisfaction and flagellation in the Sherborne Missal, see Nichols, *Seeable Signs*, p. 236. On the other hand, the scene is also a theatrically effective piece of work. Good Deeds regains her strength as Everyman beats himself ever harder — a bit of simple theater "magic" and one place to argue for the text as a real playscript.

569   *ye wyll saved be*. This conditional promise by Confession has been taken as a signifying absolution (Cawley, p. 33), the third part of the Sacrament of Penance, though the words of absolution are missing and the fourth part, satisfaction, is yet to come. See also Discretion's promise at line 693 "That all shall be well."

572   *Oyle of Forgyvenes*. Promised to Adam in legend and subsequently identified with God's mercy as extended through the Savior; see Conley, "The Phrase 'the Oyle of Forgyuenes' in 'Everyman'." Cawley had argued for seeing the "Oyle of Forgyvenes" as a reference to the rite of Extreme Unction (p. 34).

589   *Raunsomer and Redemer*. Reference to the ransom theory of atonement in which the Devil was held to have been given rights over human souls on account of the

Fall of Adam; this condition required Jesus to be sacrificed in order to ransom the souls of his people, including the faithful who lived prior to his incarnation. These were released from Hell at the Harrowing, just as ordinary Christians will be saved ultimately, even if necessarily after a period of time in Purgatory, described at line 618 as "that sharpe fyre" in the Pynson fragment and the Huntington text of *Everyman*.

596   *Moyses table*. The two tables of the Law were interpreted as representing Baptism and Penance. This is an alteration of the meaning of the Dutch text, which refers to the book of life; see Wood, "*Elckerlijc–Everyman*," p. 292.

597–98   *Mary, pray . . . / Me for to helpe at my endynge*. Invoking the Virgin Mary to mediate between the individual and her Son was held to be effective, since the Son would be especially responsive to the mother. The Hail Mary added to the biblical text the words "Mother of God, pray for us sinners now and in the hour of our death."

599   *my enemy*. The Devil.

614   *delytest to go gaye and fresshe*. Fashionably dressed, in bright colors. Cooper and Wortham, citing the Wife of Bath's Tale in which the wife says her fifth husband was "fressh and gay" — i.e., sexually proficient and alluring — suggest an erotic connotation (p. 40). But principally such clothing denotes pride. This reference again sharpens the reference to recklessness traceable to the body.

615   *the waye of dampnacyon*. As opposed to the way of salvation. These are the two paths which humans may travel. The one avoided here is the "primrose way to th' everlasting bonfire" (*Macbeth* 2.3.19).

617   *I wyll wade the water clere*. Penance reaffirms the cleansing effect of one's baptism.

618   *from Hell and from the fyre*. This reading differs from the Huntington print and the Pynson fragment, which have "Purgatory and that sharpe fyre." It would be hard to argue for a Protestant reading here, however, since the understanding of Priesthood and the Sacraments in the Huth text remains firmly Catholic, and this kind of extreme punishment was also believed to be present in Purgatory, albeit without condemnation to such suffering for eternity, as in Hell. Protestants of course rejected the idea of Purgatory.

619   *now I can walke and go*. Confession and Penance have had a healing effect as made visible through the ability of his Good Deeds to achieve health, to be delivered from "wo" (depression), and to rise up, stand, and walk. (See the beginning of Chaucer's Parson's Tale with its admonition from Jeremias 6:5 and 6:10 to arise, stand, see, walk, and find.) Good Deeds are meritorious toward salvation only when one's sins are forgiven through these rites. In *Elckerlijc*, Virtue is explicitly returned to health.

623   *be mery and gladde*. Everyman has overcome despair, and, as line 627 says, his heart is permanently "lyght" and therefore free.

643   *garmente of Sorowe*. The garment of Contrition could have been made of rough, undyed cloth, in contrast to the fashionable clothes that Everyman had worn up

to this point (see line 614). However, Craik *(Tudor Interlude,* p. 79) more plausibly offers the suggestion that it was a penitential robe of white that public penitents were required to put on. Such a change of costume, representing transformation of character, was conventional, but here would have, as Craik notes, the additional value of representing the shroud worn by Everyman when he subsequently enters the grave. The theological point is more clearly presented in *Elckerlijc*, which calls it a "garment of Remorse."

660   *Dyscressyon.* The Dutch words *wijsheit* and *vroetscap* could be translated as "wisdom," but Prudence is preferable as it adds experience, or common sense, to wisdom. This is consistent with Discretion in *Everyman*, but see also the explanatory note to line 686, below.

686   *FIVE WITS.* These are sight, hearing, smell, taste, and feeling, which are conveniently listed in *The Worlde and the Chylde,* lines 888–90, alongside the "other" five (spiritual) wits (lines 894–97). Discretion is the faculty of judgment applied to the Five Wits, and hence discriminates between true and false sensory perceptions. Conley, "Identity of Discretion in *Everyman,*" identifies the term with Prudence. In the play it is a translation from the Dutch *Vroetscap.*

687   *for swete nor soure.* Whether things turn out well or badly.

699   *In almes half my good.* For the importance of charity for salvation, see Introduction, pp. 8–9. That a rich man might give half his property to charity would not have been unusual.

701–02   *the other halfe . . . / In quyet to be returned there it ought to be.* Half his property is to be returned by way of a bequest to rightful owners. Restitution is, like giving to charity, necessary for Everyman's account book to be set straight. *Everyman* uses the appropriate legal terminology that is missing in *Elckerlijc.*

707   *Pryesthode.* Subsequent lines, spoken by Five Wits, set forth the Catholic view of the Sacraments and the priest's role in administering them as well as the doctrine of transubstantiation, the late medieval view of the elements of the Eucharist as changed into "Goddes precyous flesshe and blode" (line 724) under the forms of bread and wine. This view is reiterated at lines 737–39.

717   *He bereth the keyes.* See explanatory note to line 487, above. In *Elckerlijc,* the singular "slotel" designates the power to forgive sins.

719–20   *God for our soules medycyne / Gave us out of his harte with great pyne.* Referring specifically to Christ's blood, given during his Crucifixion, which is identified with the Eucharistic act that reenacts his sacrifice "in this transytory lyfe for thee and me" (line 721); hence the Crucifixion becomes an event contemporary with the person who sees or partakes of the elements. Not uncommonly in late medieval depictions of the Crucifixion do we see angels with chalices collecting the blood flowing from the Savior's wounds.

725   *Penaunce.* This Sacrament had been omitted from the corresponding passage in *Elckerlijc* and, as Cawley notes (p. 36), is oddly placed at the end here whereas traditionally it was third or fourth in the listing of Sacraments.

728   *Fayne wolde I receyve that holy body*. Everyman will receive only the bread, which in the rite is believed to have been transformed into the body of Christ; in Roman Catholic practice, the cup was reserved for the clergy until the Second Vatican Council.

737   *With five wordes*. The words of consecration in the Canon of the Mass are "Hoc est enim Corpus meum" ("This is my body"), derived from Luke 22:19.

740   *byndeth and unbyndeth*. The priest's power to bind and loose sins. See explanatory note to line 487, above.

744   *surgyon that cureth synne deedly*. As mediators between God and penitents, priests function as physicians to cure the disease of deadly sin. See also explanatory note on lines 719–20, above.

747   *God gave pryest that dygnyté*. The power of the keys; see explanatory note to line 487, above.

749   *above angelles in degré*. Bevington (*Tudor Drama and Politics*, p. 36) cites Thomas à Kempis, *Imitation of Christ* 4.5: "Grand is this Mystery; great too is the dignity of the Priests, to whom has been granted that which is not permitted to Angels. For none but Priests duly ordained in the Church, have power to celebrate this Sacrament, and to consecrate the Body of Christ." Thomas likewise sees priests above the angels (ibid., 4.11), an idea that also may be found in a quotation attributed to St. John Chrysostom in a sermon in British Library MS Royal 18.B.xxiii (*Middle English Sermons*, ed. Ross): "This office of presthod ther myght never pure man ordeyn, nothur aungell, nothur archaungell. . . . And so perfite [God] mad presthode that never non aungell atteyned to so high perfite an office" (p. 280).

750–63   This criticism of unworthy priests also appeared in *Elckerlijc*, and represents a common complaint of the time which after 1517 led to the Protestant Reformation's condemnation of indulgences and sacerdotal celibacy. Disapproval of the sale of indulgences, simony, and sexual abuses was not a preserve of Protestantism, however, since such behavior was at that time found at the highest levels of the hierarchy.

753   *same Sacrament*. Cawley (p. 36) supposes an error, since *Elckerlijc* has "Sacramenten seven." In their edition of *Everyman*, Conley et al. emend the text to "seven sacramentes." Cooper and Wortham point out, however, that "same Sacrament" is credible as the "one great Sacrament, the institution of the Church as the Mystical Body of Christ," from which "the seven individual sacraments ensued" (*Summoning of Everyman*, p. 48).

755–57   *Saynt Peter the apostle . . . do bye or sell*. Denunciation of simony. See Acts 8:18–24.

767   *shepe . . . shepeherdes*. Conventional metaphor for clergy and laypeople; see John 10:1–28.

770   *satysfaccyon*. See explanatory notes to lines 561 and 569, above. Everyman has now completed his penance, which began with contrition.

778   *Rodde*. Persons about to expire were advised to keep focused on a crucifix (rood), according to treatises on dying. However, Wood, "*Elckerlijc–Everyman*," p. 279, suggested that a pilgrim's staff (*rod*) might be meant, though he notes that *Humulus*, a Latin translation of the play, offered the word *crucem*.

787   *Judas Machabé*. Judas Maccabeus, one of the Nine Worthies, recognized as powerful men in history. Conley, "Reference to Judas Maccabeus," however, points to the Nine Worthies as symbols of the vanity of the world — and hence the reference to this figure is appropriate for Strength, who in spite of his protests will desert Everyman only a few lines later. The author of *Everyman* has added the name here for the sake of rhyme.

793   *turne to erth*. In addition to the Ash Wednesday liturgy ("Remember, man, that you are earth and to earth you shall return"), see also the popular poem *Erthe upon Erthe* (ed. Murray). A version of this poem appeared in a wall painting at Statford-upon-Avon in conjunction with a representation of the Dance of Death; see Davidson, *Guild Chapel Wall Paintings at Stratford-upon-Avon*, pp. 30, 48–49, fig. 14.

801   *I take my tappe in my lap*. Bevington, *Medieval Drama*, p. 960, glosses: "I'll gather up my spinning and be on my way." In addition to flax on a distaff, the word "tappe" may simply mean "a bundle of combed wool prepared for spinning" (*OED*). The reading *cap* of the Huth print seems to be an error. The reference to an apparent stage property in *Everyman* does not appear in *Elckerlijc*.

803   *I loke not behynde me*. The Dutch text literally reads "I polish my behind." The meaning is that Beauty's promise is retracted.

804   *and thou wolde gyve me all the golde in thy chest*. In iconography, the wealth of the dying man could be represented as a chest at the foot of his bed; see the Introduction, pp. 5–6, for reference to Hieronymus Bosch's *Death of the Miser*. Hence this can be read as "If you give me all the gold that you have accumulated" — less extravagant than the Dutch play's "all the world's riches." Logically, of course, Beauty must be left behind at death, as also will be his Strength, Discretion, Five Wits, and, at the last, Knowledge, who is not able to pass into the grave with Everyman. See lines 862–63, for Knowledge's promise not to leave Everyman until "I se where ye shall become" — i.e., if he successfully passes into the life after death.

817   *Ye be olde ynough*. Sarcasm.

828   *She*. Strength as a feminine personification is an oddity. A male is represented in the factotum woodcut in the Huth edition (sig. A1v) showing the characters in the play. In the extant fragment *The Pride of Life*, Strength is presented as a knight who challenges Death.

843   *whan Deth bloweth his blaste*. The sound of the trumpet. This instrument is associated with Judgment, especially the Last Judgment, when angels were believed to be prepared to sound their trumpets. But there were variants of this iconography. Devils attempt to blow horns in the Doomsday wall painting at Stratford-upon-Avon; see Davidson, *Guild Chapel Wall Paintings*, fig. 17. In Con-

tinental examples, Death also might be shown blowing a horn; see Briese-meister, *Bilder des Todes*, figs. 1, 3, 32, 34, 38.

850   *and there an ende*. Proverbial; see Dent, E113.1.

852   *I wyll byde wyth thee*. Good Deeds will prove to be the only friend to abide with Everyman unto his judgment before the high seat of Heaven, even though he had loved all the others (as listed in lines 871–72) better.

863   *Tyll I se where ye shall become*. See explanatory note to line 804, above.

867   *all ye that this do here or se*. Hearing and seeing imply actual stage production, but this line is directly translated from *Elkerlijc* and hence cannot be cited as proof with regard to the English play. Everyman's admonition to the audience seems modeled on the *O vos omnes* tradition of Christ's speech to bystanders from the Cross; for an example, see Browne, *Religious Lyrics of the Fifteenth Century*, pp. 151–56. See also the discussion in Woolf, *English Religious Lyric in the Middle Ages*, pp. 40–45.

870   *All erthly thynge is but vanyté*. See Ecclesiastes 12:8: "all things are vanity."

875   *stande by me thou moder and mayde, holy Mary*. See note to lines 597–98, above. According to the doctrine of her perpetual virginity, Mary is a maid, or virgin, though she is married to Joseph, conventionally depicted as an old (and impotent) man. See the antiphon *Alma redemptoris mater*, the song of the "litel clergeon" in the Prologue to Chaucer's Prioress' Tale: "You who, while nature wondered, gave birth to your own sacred Creator and yet remained a virgin afterward as before" (text, translation, and transcription of the Sarum rite music in Davidson, *Substance and Manner*, p. 22).

876   *I wyll speke for thee*. Good deeds, especially the Corporal Acts of Mercy, are the distinguishing factor at the judgment of the individual by God. Depictions of the Last Judgment occasionally included the traditional iconographic motif of the weighing of souls on a set of scales, sometimes with the Virgin Mary helping to tip the scales to the person's benefit by placing a rosary on it to counteract his or her bad deeds. See Perry, "On the Psychostasis in Christian Art — II," p. 215.

880   *Into thy handes, Lord, my soule I commende*. In imitation of Jesus, echoing his dying words on the Cross, according to Luke 23:46. The Latin text is recited in lines 886–87 as Everyman is about to enter the grave with Good Deeds. For a similar case of a dying man speaking the Latin text, see *The Rohan Master: A Book of Hours*, pl. 63. Rastall, "Music and Liturgy in *Everyman*," p. 308, points out that "these words belong to the additional verses said following the office of Extreme Unction." They are also recommended in the *ars moriendi* texts; see Beaty, *Craft of Dying*, p. 21.

885   *saved at the Dome*. Everyman's soul is now directly facing the particular Judgment, to be followed at the end of history by the general Judgment when all must appear before God to be dispersed to Heaven or to Hell.

891   *I here angelles synge*. *Veni electa mea* and *Veni de libano sponsa mea* are perhaps the best candidates for the item to be sung here since these are the alternatives

suggested by line 894; other possibilities are listed by Rastall, "Music and Liturgy in *Everyman*," p. 309. *Veni electa mea* was used in the York Assumption play, and, since it alludes to the Song of Songs, this is one of the available items appropriate for "the soul's mystical marriage to Christ," as Cowling suggests ("Angels' Song in *Everyman*," p. 302).

894   *Cume, excellent electe spouse.* See explanatory note to line 891, above, and compare the Angel's speech in *Elckerlijc*.

895   *Here above.* Further verification that the location for Heaven was to be thought of as raised above the playing area.

897   *Now thy soule is taken thy body fro.* If the body has entered into the grave, how the soul is subsequently to appear to be separated from the body is unclear. In the visual arts, the soul is often a small doll-like figure that is taken from the dying man's mouth at his last breath. In the Carthusian Miscellany (British Library MS 37,049, fol. 29), for example, the soul of the dying man is saved by an angel, who rescues it from a waiting devil, who in turn expresses his anger at the loss in the accompanying text. For a brief discussion of the iconography, see Rogers, "Particular Judgement," pp. 125–27.

899   *Now shalt thou into the hevenly spere.* The text in the Carthusian Miscellany that accompanies the angel's rescue promises the dying man that he will "bere thi saule to blis on hye" (British Library MS 37,049, fol. 29r).

901   *Day of Dome.* Last Judgment, at the end of history. Following this line, Rastall, "Music and Liturgy in *Everyman*," p. 311, suggests music as the angel takes Everyman's soul up to Heaven, probably in a napkin as in a conventional iconography (e.g., in a tomb sculpture at Ely Cathedral or, for a Continental example, on an altarpiece attributed to Simon Marmion, both illustrated in Boase, *Death in the Middle Ages*, figs. 29, 31).

902   DOCTOR. In *Everyman*, the epilogue is assigned to the Doctor (of theology or philosophy), who speaks of the play as a "memoryall" (but called a "morall" only in the Huntington print). The object has been to construct a drama that will call to mind the existential realities of life lived between deadly sin (Pride, which in some sense encompasses all the Seven Deadly Sins) and the necessity for charitable works (Good Deeds), which are one's only true friends.

912   *after deth amendes may no man make.* The time of mercy is past, as line 913 indicates.

915   *Ite maledicti in ignem eternum.* "Go, wicked ones, into the eternal fire"; see Matthew 25:41, Jesus' condemnation of those who have failed to do the Corporal Acts of Mercy and who hence will be consigned to Hell. Compare Matthew 25:30, which similarly damns the "unprofitable servant" in the parable of the talents to "the exterior darkness" where "there shall be weeping and gnashing of teeth."

917   *Hye in Heven he shall be crounde.* In Heaven the souls of the righteous will receive crowns.

919   *body and soule togyther*. For the resurrection of the body, see the Nicene Creed.

922   *Amen*. Rastall, "Music and Liturgy in *Everyman*," p. 311, suggests the possibility
         of the audience joining the cast in saying "Amen" at the end of the play. In the
         Dutch text, it will be noted, "Amen" preceded the Epilogue.

TEXTUAL NOTES TO *EVERYMAN*

Only the principal variants from the copytext (Huth 32) are given here. Complete bibliographic information for the editions cited in the list of abbreviations below appears in the Select Bibliography.

ABBREVIATIONS: BL: British Library C.21.c.17; **Cawley**: *Everyman*, ed. Cawley (rpt. 1977); **Douce**: Douce Fragment, Bodleian Library; **Hunt**: Huntington Library copy; **Huth**: British Library, Huth 32.

14	*thy soule*. So Huth. Hunt: *the soule*.
29	*lawe*. So Huth, Hunt. Cawley: *love*.
30	*so*. So Huth. Hunt omits.
31	*cannot*. So Hunt. Huth: *caunot*.
41	*not*. So Huth. Hunt: *nothynge*.
73	*cruelly*. So Hunt. Huth: *truely*.
77	*depart*. So Huth. Hunt: *to departe*.
109	*spente*. So Hunt. Huth: *spede*.
111	*ado that thou*. So Cawley. Huth: *ado that we*; Hunt: *I do we*.
113	*rekenynge*. So Hunt. Huth: *rekenyuge*.
119	*whan*. So Hunt. Huth: *what*.
129	*All*. So Huth. Hunt: *But*.
135	*twelve*. Huth, Hunt: *.xii.*
141	*thee*. Huth: *the*; Hunt: *that*.
168	*Everyman*. So Hunt. Huth: *Euenyman*.
	mad, that. So Huth. Hunt: *made thou*.
180	*out of*. So Huth. Hunt: *out of thy*.
205	*good Felawshyp*. So Hunt. Huth: *god felawshyp*.
248	*dutye*. Huth: *duyte*; Hunt: *duty*.
252	*here as*. So Huth. Hunt: *here as well as*.
260	*agayne cume*. So Cawley. Huth: *cume agayne*; Hunt: *come agayne*.
278	*to folye wyll*. So Huth. Hunt: *wyll*.
300	omit FELLOWSHIP (misplaced in Huth).
301	*FELLOWSHIP*. So Hunt. Huth: *EVERYMAN*.
	endynge. So Cawley. Huth, Hunt: *ende*.
303	*EVERYMAN*. So Hunt. Huth omits.
317	*them*. So Cawley. Huth, Hunt, BL: *them go*.
327	*Gramercy*. So Hunt, BL. Huth: *Geamercy*.
365	*Now*. So Hunt. BL: *Nowe*; Huth: *Nw*.

375	*my owne.* So Huth. Hunt: *myne owne*; BL: *myne owne lyfe.*
390	*It.* So Huth, BL. Hunt: *He.*
401	*trouble.* So Huth. Hunt, BL: *sorowe.*
406	*gyve.* So Hunt, BL. Huth: *gyne.*
415	*vyages.* Greg notes possibly *vyages longe.*
432	*of.* So Hunt. Huth: *for*; BL: *for the love of.*
436	*my spendynge.* So Huth, Hunt. BL: *myspending.*
442	*condycyon.* So Hunt. BL: *condition*; Huth: *condycyons.*
455	*gladde.* So Huth, Hunt. BL: *right gladde.*
457	*longe.* So Hunt. Huth omits.
475	*into.* So Hunt, BL. Huth: *in.*
489	*feare.* So Huth. Hunt: *fere*; BL: *great feare.*
504	*Beholde.* So Huth. Hunt, BL: *Ase.*
527	*she.* Huth, Hunt, BL: *he.*
530	*at.* So Hunt, BL. Huth: *at the.*
538	*you.* So Hunt, BL. Huth: *yon.*
	instructe me by intelleccyon. So Huth. Hunt: *gyve me cognycyon*; BL: *gyve me cognisyon.*
539	*man.* So Hunt, BL. Huth: *vertue.*
549	*Repent . . . full.* So BL. Hunt: *Redempte . . . full*; Huth: *Redempe . . . full of.*
565	*scape that paynful.* So Huth, Hunt. BL: *passe thy.*
566	*Knowlege, kepe hym.* So Hunt, BL. Huth: *Knowlege hym and kepe hym.*
568	*sure.* So Huth. Hunt, BL: *seker.*
580	*clerely.* So Hunt, BL. Huth: *crelery.*
594	*unworthy.* So Hunt, BL. Omit Huth.
	of thy benygnyté. So Huth. Hunt, BL: *in this hevy lyfe.*
602	*partetaker.* So Huth. Hunt: *partynere*; BL: *partinere.*
603	*meanes.* So Hunt. Huth, BL: *meane.*
606	*gyve acqueyntaunce.* So Hunt. Huth: *gyve a quytaunce.* BL: *have aquaintaunce.*
610	*Now.* So Hunt. BL: *Nowe*; Huth: *Thus.*
615	*the.* So Hunt, BL. Huth omits.
616	*and.* So Huth. Hunt, BL: *of.*
618	*Hell and from the.* So Huth. Hunt: *purgatory and that sharpe*; BL: *purgatory that sharpe.*
622	*good.* So Hunt, BL. Huth: *god.*
624	*do come.* So Huth. Hunt: *cometh now*; BL: *commeth nowe.*
640	*Lest . . . it be unswete.* So Huth. Hunt: *Or elles . . . you may it mysse*; BL: *Or els . . . ye may it misse.*
656	KNOWLEDGE. So Cawley. Huth, Hunt: KINDRED; BL: KINDREDE.
666	KNOWLEDGE. So Cawley. Huth, Hunt: KINDRED; BL: KINDREDE.
670	*redy.* So Huth, BL. Hunt: *all redy.*
692	*vertuous.* So Hunt, BL, Douce. Huth: *vertues.*
702	*In quyet.* So Huth. Hunt: *In queth*; BL, Douce: *I it bequethe.*
716	*benygne.* So Hunt, Douce. BL: *benigne*; Huth: *benynge.*
717	*he cure.* So Huth. Hunt: *the cure*; BL, Douce: *cure.*
726	*seven.* Huth, Hunt, BL, Douce: *.vii.*
732	*good Pryesthod.* So Huth. Hunt, BL, Douce: *preesthode.*

737	*five*. Huth, Hunt, BL, Douce: *.v.*
738	*make*. So Huth, Hunt. BL, Douce: *take*.
746	*all onely*. So Huth, Hunt. BL, Douce: *alone on*.
770	*satysfaccyon*. So Hunt. BL: *satisfaction*; Huth: *satysfaccoon*.
774	*than*. So Hunt. Huth: *thou*. BL omits.
782	*gone*. So Huth, BL, Douce. Hunt: *done*.
786	STRENGTH. So BL. Huth, Hunt, Douce omit.
793	*to erth*. So Hunt. Huth: *to the erth*; BL, Douce: *to the erthe*.
801	*tappe*. So Hunt, BL. Huth: *cap*.
806	*goeth . . . and from me*. So Huth. Hunt: *gothe . . . fro me*; Douce: *gothe . . . and hye*; BL: *dothe . . . hye*.
827	*He that*. So Huth, Hunt, Douce. BL: *But I se well he that*.
828	*She hym deceyveth*. So Huth, Hunt, Douce. BL: *Is greatly disceyved*.
829	*Bothe . . . forsaketh me*. So Hunt. Huth, Douce: *Both . . . forsaketh me*; BL: *For . . . hath forsaken me*.
830	*fayre and lovyngly*. So Huth, Hunt, Douce. BL: *stedfast to be*.
838	*ones pyteously*. So Huth, Hunt. Douce: *ones petyously*; BL: *and thou shalt se*.
854	*good*. So Hunt, BL, Douce. Huth: *god*.
855	*Dedes*. So Hunt, BL, Douce. Huth: *Dede*.
870	*erthly*. Hunt, Douce. Huth: *ertly*; BL: *erthely*.
885	*Dome*. So Huth, Douce. Hunt, BL: *Day of Dome*.
902	*memoryall*. So Huth, BL, Douce. Hunt: *morall*.
914	*rekenynge*. So Hunt, Douce. BL: *rekening*; Huth: *rekenyuge*.
915	*eternum*. So Hunt, BL, Douce. Huth: *eternam*.
921	*Say ye*. So Huth. Hunt, BL, Douce: *Amen saye ye*.
922	*Amen*. So Huth. Hunt, BL, Douce: *Finis*.

APPENDIX: THE GOLDEN LEGEND

The Christianized Buddhist parable of the false friends as it appeared in Jacobus de Voragine's *Golden Legend* was the best-known version of the story in the Low Countries and England in the late fifteenth and early sixteenth centuries. In William Caxton's translation it appeared as one of the stories in "The Lyf of Saynt Balaam the Heremyte" amongst the saints' lives preserved in this collection. The text that appears below is from the 1493 edition issued by Wynkyn de Worde (*Short-Title Catalogue*, no. 24875). The quoted passage follows another parable of a man fleeing from a unicorn and falling into "a grete pyte" in which a "an horryble dragon castyng fyre" lurked with "his mouth opene" at the bottom. Hanging from a tree branch and with his feet on a small and insecure ledge, he observed two mice (one black, one white) gnawing away at the tree's roots. But when he saw honey hanging "in the bowes of the tree," he "forgate the perylle that he was in," "gave hym all to the swetenesse of that lytyll hony," and became indifferent to his danger. In the explication of the parable, the unicorn is Death and the dragon is "the mouth of helle, whiche desyreth to devoure alle creatures." The pit is this world, and the mice, representing the hours of night and day, are Time as the destroyer, attacking the "tree of the lyf of every man." The honey's sweetness, in turn, is "the false deceyvable delectacion of the worlde, by whiche man is deceyved, soo that he taketh noo hede of the perylle that he is in" (fols. 344r–344v). At this point Balaam (i.e., Barlaam) begins the parable of the false friends:

> And yet he sayde that they that love the world ben semblable to a man that had
> thre frendes, of whiche he loved the fyrste as moche as hi[m]self; and he lovyd the
> seconde lasse thenne hymself, and loved the thyrde a lytyll or nought. It happed
> soo that this man was in grete perylle of his lyf and was somoned before the kyng.
> 5 Thenne he ranne to hys fyrste frende and demaunded of him his helpe and tolde
> to hym how he hadde alwaye lovyd him; to whom he sayde: "I have other frendes
> wyth whom I must be this day, and I wote not who thou art: therfore I maye not
> helpe thee. Yet neverthelesse I shall give to thee two sloppes wyth whiche thou
> mayst cover thee."
> 10 And thenne he wente awaye moche sorowfull, and went to that other frende
> and requyred also his ayde. And he sayd to hym, "I may not attende to goo wyth
> thee to this debate; for I have grete charge, but I shal yet felawshyp thee unto the
> gate of the paleys, and thenne I shal retourne agayn and do myn owne nedes."
> And thenne he, beyng hevy and as despayred, went to the thyrde frende and
> 15 sayd to hym: "I have noo reson to speke to thee, ne, I have not loved thee as I

1 **semblable**, akin. **3 happed**, happened. **8 sloppes**, loose outer garments. **12 felawshyp**, accompany. **15 ne**, no (truly not).

oughte, but I am in trybulacion and without frendes, and praye thee that thou
15   helpe me." And that other sayd wyth glad chere, "Certes, I confesse to be thy dere
frende and have not foryeten thee, lytyll benefayte that thou hast done to me. I
shall goo ryght gladly wyth thee tofore the kynge for to see what shall be de-
maunded of thee, and I shall praye the kynge for thee."

The fyrste frende is possession of rychesse, for whiche man putteth hym in
20   many peryllys, and whan the Deth cometh, he hath no more of it but a cloth for to
wynde hym for to be buryed. The seconde frende is his sones, hys wyf, and kynne,
whiche goo wyth hym to his grave, and anone retourne for to entende to theyr
owne nedes. The thyrde frende is fayth, hope, and charyté and other good werkys
whiche we have done, that whan we yssue out of oure bodyes, they may well goo
25   tofore us and praye God for us; and they maye well delyver us fro the devyllis our
enemyes. (fol. 344r)

16 foryeten, forgotten. **22 entende**, attend.

# BIBLIOGRAPHY

Adolf, Helen. "From *Everyman* and *Elckerlijc* to Hofmannsthal and Kafka." *Comparative Literature* 9, no. 3 (1957): 204–14.

Anderson, M. D. *Drama and Imagery in English Medieval Churches*. Cambridge: Cambridge University Press, 1963.

The Art and Crafte to Knowe Well to Dye. London: William Caxton, 1490.

Audelay, John. *The Poems*. Ed. Ella Keats Whiting. EETS o.s. 184. London: Oxford University Press, 1931.

Augustine. *On Christian Doctrine*. Trans. D. W. Robertson. Indianapolis: Bobbs-Merrill, 1958.

Barlam and Iosaphat: A Middle English Life of Buddha. Ed. John C. Hirsch. EETS o.s. 290. Oxford: Oxford University Press, 1986.

———. *Barlaam and Josaphat: A Transcription of MS Egerton 876, with Notes, Glossary, and Comparative Study of the Middle English and Japanese Versions*. Ed. Keiko Ikegami. New York: AMS Press, 1999.

Beaty, Nancy Lee. *The Craft of Dying: A Study in the Literary Tradition of the Ars Moriendi in England*. New Haven: Yale University Press, 1970.

Bennett, H. S. *English Books and Readers, 1475 to 1557*. Second ed. Cambridge: Cambridge University Press, 1969.

Bergman, Ingmar. *Four Screen Plays*. Trans. Lars Malmstrom and David Kushner. New York: Simon and Schuster, 1960.

Bevington, David. *From* Mankind *to Marlowe: Growth of Structure in the Popular Drama of Tudor England*. Cambridge, MA: Harvard University Press, 1962.

———. *Tudor Drama and Politics: A Critical Approach to Topical Meaning*. Cambridge, MA: Harvard University Press, 1968.

———. *Medieval Drama*. See *Everyman*.

Boase, T. S. R. *Death in the Middle Ages; Mortality, Judgement and Remembrance*. London: Thames and Hudson, 1972.

Briesemeister, Dietrich. *Bilder des Todes*. Unterscheidheim: Verlag Walter Uhl, 1970.

Browne, Carleton Fairchild, ed. *Religious Lyrics of the Fifteenth Century*. Oxford: Clarendon Press, 1939.

Browne, E. Martin, and Henzie R. Browne. *Two in One*. Cambridge: Cambridge University Press, 1981.

Carruthers, Mary. *The Book of Memory: A Study of Memory in Medieval Culture*. Cambridge: Cambridge University Press, 1990.

The Castle of Perseverance. See *The Macro Plays*.

Chaucer, Geoffrey. *The Riverside Chaucer*. Third ed. Gen ed. Larry D. Benson. Boston: Houghton Mifflin, 1987.

Chaundler, Thomas. *Liber Apologeticus de Omni Statu Humanae Naturae*. Ed. Doris Enright-Clark Shoukri. London: Modern Humanities Research Association, 1974.

Cheetham, Francis. *English Medieval Alabasters: With a Catalogue of the Collection in the Victoria and Albert Museum*. Oxford: Phaidon-Christie's, 1984.

Clark, James M. *The Dance of Death in the Middle Ages and Renaissance*. Glasgow: Jackson, 1950.

Cole, Wendel. "Elizabethan Stages and Open-Air Stages in America a Half Century Ago." *Quarterly Journal of Speech* 47 (1961): 41–50.

Coleridge, Samuel Taylor. *Statesman's Manual.* In *The Complete Works.* Ed. W. G. T. Shedd. 7 vols. New York: Harper, 1884.

Collier, John Payne. *The History of English Dramatic Poetry to the Time of Shakespeare, and Annals of the Stage to the Restoration.* 3 vols. 1831. Rpt. New York: AMS Press, 1970.

Conley, John. "The Reference to Judas Maccabeus in 'Everyman.'" *Notes and Queries* 212 (1967): 50–51.

———."The Doctrine of Friendship in *Everyman.*" *Speculum* 44 (1969): 374–82.

———. "The Phrase 'the Oyle of Forgyuenes' in 'Everyman': A Reference to Extreme Unction?" *Notes and Queries* 220 (1975): 105–06.

———. "The Identity of Discretion in *Everyman.*" *Notes and Queries* 228 (1983): 394–96.

———. "'If ye had parfytely chered me': The Nurturing of Good Deeds in *Everyman.*" *Notes and Queries* 240 (1995): 166–67.

Cowling, Douglas. "The Angels' Song in *Everyman.*" *Notes and Queries* 233 (1988): 301–03.

Craik, T. W. *The Tudor Interlude: Stage, Costume and Acting.* Leicester: Leicester University Press, 1958.

Cross, F. L., and E. A. Livingstone, eds. *The Oxford Dictionary of the Christian Church.* Third ed. Oxford: Oxford University Press, 1997.

Cunningham, John. "Comedic and Liturgical Restoration in *Everyman.*" *Comparative Drama* 22 (1988): 162–73.

The Dance of Death. See Lydgate, John.

Davidson, Audrey. *Substance and Manner: Studies in Music and the Other Arts.* St. Paul, MN: Hiawatha Press, 1977.

Davidson, Clifford. *The Guild Chapel Wall Paintings at Stratford-upon-Avon.* New York: AMS Press, 1987.

———. *Visualizing the Moral Life: Medieval Iconography and the Macro Morality Plays.* New York: AMS Press, 1989.

———. *Illustrations of the Stage and Acting in England to 1580.* Kalamazoo, MI: Medieval Institute Publications, 1991.

———. "Repentance and the Fountain: The Transformation of Symbols in English Emblem Books." In *The Art of the Emblem: Essays in Honor of Karl Josef Höltgen.* Ed. Michael Bath et al. New York: AMS Press, 1993. Pp. 5–37.

———. "Saint Plays and Pageants of Medieval Britain." *Early Drama, Art, and Music Review* 22, no. 1 (1999): 11–37.

de Geus, B., et al., eds. *Een scone Leeringe om salich te sterven: Een Middelnederlandse ars moriendi.* Utrecht: HES, 1985.

Dent, R. W. *Proverbial Language in English Drama exclusive of Shakespeare, 1495–1616: An Index.* Berkeley: University of California Press, 1984.

Douglas, Audrey, and Peter Greenfield, eds. *Records of Early English Drama: Cumberland, Westmorland, Gloucestershire.* Toronto: University of Toronto Press, 1986.

Dugdale, William. *The History of St. Pauls Cathedral in London From its Foundation Untill These Times Extracted Out of Originall Charters, Records, Leiger Books, and Other Manuscripts: Beautified with Sundry Prospects of the Church, Figures of Tombs and Monuments.* London: Tho. Warren, 1658.

Early English Miscellanies in Prose and Verse. Ed. J. O. Halliwell-Phillipps. London: Warton Club, 1855.

The Early English Versions of the Gesta Romanorum. Ed. Sidney Herrtage. EETS e.s. 33. London: N. Trübner, 1879.

Elckerlijc. In *Elckerlijk, a Fifteenth Century Dutch Morality, and Everyman, a Nearly Contemporary Translation.* Ed. Henri Logeman. Gand: Librairie Clemm, 1892.

———. In *Den Spyeghel der Salicheyt van Elckerlijc.* Ed. Kornelis H. De Raaf and Petrus Dorlandus. Groningen: P. Noordhoff, 1897.

———. In *Elckerlyc-Studiën.* Ed. Leonard Willems. The Hague: M. Nijhoff, 1934.

———. In *Vijf Geestelijke Toneelspelen der Middeleeuwen.* Ed. H. J. E. Endepols. Amsterdam: Elsevier, 1940.

———. In *Elckerlijc, Nieuwe bijdragen met geëmendeerde uitgave*. Ed. J. van Mierlo. Turnhout: Van Mierlo-Proost, 1949.

———. In *Den Spyeghel der Salicheyt van Elckerlijc*. Ed. H. J. E. Endepols. Sixth ed. Groningen: J. B. Wolters, 1955.

———. In *Den Spieghel der Salicheit van Elckerlijc*. Ed. R. Vos. Groningen: J. B. Wolters, 1967.

———. In *The Mirror of Salvation: A Moral Play of Everyman, c. 1490*. Trans. Adriaan J. Barnouw. The Hague: Martinus Nijhoff, 1971.

———. In *De Spiegel der Zaligheid van Elkerlijk*. Ed. M. J. M. de Haan and B. J. van Delden. Leiden: Vakgroep Nederlandse Taal- & Letterkunde, 1979.

———. In *Den Spyeghel der Salicheyt van Elckerlijc*. Ed. A. Van Elslander. Eighth ed. Antwerp: Nederlandsche Boekhandel, 1985.

———. In *The Mirror of Everyman's Salvation: A Prose Translation of the Original Everyman*. Ed. and trans. John Conley, Guido de Baere, H. J. C. Schaap, and W. H. Toppen. Amsterdam: Rodopi, 1985.

———. In *Mariken van Nieumeghen & Elckerlijc*. Ed. and trans. [into Modern Dutch] Bart Ramakers and Willem Wilmink. Amsterdam: Prometheus/Bert Bakker, 1998.

Elliott, John. *Playing God: Medieval Mysteries on the Modern Stage*. Toronto: University of Toronto Press, 1989.

Erenstein, R. L., ed. *Een theatergeschiedenis der Nederlanden: Tien eeuwen drama en theater in Nederland en Vlaanderen*. Amsterdam: Amsterdam University Press, 1996.

Erthe upon Erthe. In *The Middle English Poem, Erthe upon Erthe, Printed from Twenty-four Manuscripts*. Ed. Hilda M. R. Murray. EETS o.s. 141. London: K. Paul, Trench, Trübner and Co., 1911.

Everyman. In *Everyman, Reprinted from the Edition by John Skot at Britwell Court*. Ed. W. W. Greg. Materialen zur Kunde des älteren Englischen Dramas 4. Louvain: Uystpruyst, 1904.

———. In *Everyman, Reprinted from the Edition by John Skot in the Possession of Mr. A. H. Huth*. Ed. W. W. Greg. Materialen zur Kunde des älteren Englischen Dramas 24. Louvain: Uystpruyst, 1909.

———. In *Everyman, Reprinted from the Fragments of Two Editions by Pynson Preserved in the Bodleian Library and the British Museum*. Ed. W. W. Greg. Materialen zur Kunde des älteren Englischen Dramas 28b. Louvain: Uystpruyst, 1910.

———. In *Medieval Drama*. Ed. David Bevington. Boston: Houghton Mifflin, 1975.

———. Ed. A. C. Cawley. 1961. Rpt., Manchester: Manchester University Press, 1977.

———. In *Everyman: A Performance Text*. Ed. John Astington. Toronto: Poculi Ludique Societas, 1980.

———. In *The Summoning of Everyman*. Ed. Geoffrey Cooper and Christopher Wortham. Nedlands: University of Western Australia Press, 1980.

———. In *Three Late Medieval Morality Plays*. Ed. G. A. Lester. New York: W. W. Norton, 1981. [Modern spelling.]

———. In *The Mirror of Everyman's Salvation*. Ed. Conley et al. See *Elckerlijc*.

———. In *Medieval Drama: An Anthology*. Ed. Greg Walker. Oxford: Blackwell, 2000.

Fletcher, Alan. "Coveytyse Copbord schal be at the Ende of the Castel by the Beddys Feet." *English Studies* 68, no. 4 (1987): 305–12.

Garner, Stanton B., Jr. "Theatricality in *Mankind* and *Everyman*." *Studies in Philology* 84, no. 3 (1987): 272–85.

Gibson, Walter S. *Hieronymus Bosch*. New York: Praeger, 1973.

Gilman, Donald, ed. *Everyman and Company: Essays on the Theme and Structure of the European Moral Play*. New York: AMS Press, 1989.

Gottfried, Robert S. *Epidemic Disease in Fifteenth Century England: The Medical Response and Demographic Consequences*. New Brunswick, NJ: Rutgers University Press, 1978.

Greenfield, Peter H. "A Processional *Everyman* at St. Martin's College." *Research Opportunities in Renaissance Drama* 32 (1993): 151–54.

———. "Census of Medieval Drama Productions." *Research Opportunities in Renaissance Drama* 37 (1998): 113-135.

Greg, W. W. *A Bibliography of the English Printed Drama to the Restoration*. 4 vols. London: Bibliographical Society, 1939–59.

Hummelen, W. M. H. "The Drama of the Dutch Rhetoricians." In *Everyman and Company: Essays on the Theme and Structure of the European Moral Play*. Ed. Donald Gilman. New York: AMS Press, 1988. Pp. 169–92.

———. "The Boundaries of the Rhetoricians' Stage." *Comparative Drama* 28 (1994): 235–51.

Illustrated Carthusian Religious Miscellany: British Library London Additional MS. 37049. Ed. James Hogg. Salzburg: Institut für Anglistik und Amerikanistik, Universität Salzburg, 1981.

Jambeck, Thomas J. "*Everyman* and the Implications of Bernardine Humanism in the Character 'Knowledge.'" *Medievalia et Humanistica*, n.s. 8 (1977): 103–23.

Johnson, Wallace H. "The Double Desertion of Everyman." *American Notes and Queries* 6 (1968): 85–87.

Kazemier, G. "Elckerlijc, Het Dal sonder Wederkeeren, en de Mystiek." *De Nieuwe Taalgids* 34 (1940): 87–96, 116–28.

King, George A. "The Pre-Reformation Painted Glass in St. Andrew's Church, Norwich." *Norfolk Archaeology* 18 (1913): 283–94.

Kölbing, E. "Kleine Beiträge zur Erklärung und Textkritik vor-Shakespeare'scher Dramen." *English Studien* 21 (1895): 170.

Kolve, V. A. "*Everyman* and the Parable of the Talents." In *Medieval English Drama: Essays Critical and Contextual*. Ed. Jerome Taylor and Alan H. Nelson. Chicago: University of Chicago Press, 1972. Pp. 316–40.

Lang, David Marshall. *The Wisdom of Balahvar: A Christian Legend of the Buddha*. New York: Macmillan, 1957.

Larsen, Erling. "All Things to Everyman." *Nuance* 2, no. 2 (1954): 30.

Little, Lester. "Pride Goes before Avarice: Social Change and Vices in Latin Christendom." *American Historical Review* 76 (1971): 16–49.

[Lydgate, John.] *The Dance of Death*, ed. Florence Warren. EETS o.s. 181. London: Oxford University Press, 1931.

Mackenzie, W. Roy. *The English Moralities from the Point of View of Allegory*. 1914. Rpt. New York: Gordian Press, 1966.

The Macro Plays. Ed. Mark Eccles. EETS o.s. 262. London: Oxford University Press, 1969.

Mâle, Émile. *Religious Art in France, the Late Middle Ages: Medieval Iconography and Its Sources*, trans. Marthiel Mathews. Princeton: Princeton University Press, 1986.

Middle English Sermons. Ed. Woodburn O. Ross. EETS o.s. 209. London: Oxford University Press, 1940.

Munson, William. "Knowing and Doing in *Everyman*." *Chaucer Review* 19, no. 3 (1985): 252–71.

Nichols, Ann Eljenholm. "Costume in the Moralities: The Evidence of East Anglian Art." *Comparative Drama* 20 (1986–87): 305–14.

———. *Seeable Signs: The Iconography of the Seven Sacraments, 1350–1544*. Woodbridge: Boydell Press, 1994.

Non-Cycle Plays and Fragments. Ed. Norman Davis. EETS s.s 1. London: Oxford University Press, 1970.

The N-Town Play. Ed. Stephen Spector. 2 vols. EETS s.s. 11–12. Oxford: Oxford University Press, 1991.

O'Connor, Marion. "*Everyman, The Creation* and *The Passion*: The Royal Shakespeare Company Medieval Season 1996–1997." *Medieval and Renaissance Drama in England* 11 (1999): 19–33.

Oosterwijk, Sophie. "Lessons in 'Hopping': The Dance of Death and the Chester Mystery Cycle." *Comparative Drama* 36 (2002–03): 249–87.

Owst, G. R. *Literature and Pulpit in Medieval England*. Second ed. 1961. Rpt. Oxford: Basil Blackwell, 1966.

Pächt, Otto, and J. J. G. Alexander. *Illuminated Manuscripts in the Bodleian Library, Oxford, 3: British, Irish, and Icelandic Schools*. Oxford: Clarendon Press, 1973.

Perry, Mary Phillips. "On the Psychostasis in Christian Art — II." *Burlington Magazine* 22 (1912): 208–18.

Phythian-Adams, Charles. *Desolation of a City: Coventry and the Urban Crisis of the Late Middle Ages*. Cambridge: Cambridge University Press, 1979.

Pickering, Kenneth. *Drama in the Cathedral: The Canterbury Festival Plays, 1928–1948*. Worthing, UK: Churchman, 1985.

Piehler, Paul. *The Visionary Landscape: A Study in Medieval Allegory*. London: Edward Arnold, 1971.

Pollard, Alfred, and G. R. Redgrave et al. *A Short-Title Catalogue of Books Printed in England, Scotland, & Ireland and of English Books Printed Abroad, 1475–1640*. London: Bibliographic Society, 1976–91.

Potter, Robert A. *The English Morality Play: Origins, History, and Influence of a Dramatic Tradition*. London: Routledge and Kegan Paul, 1975.

Pride of Life. See *Non-Cycle Plays and Fragments*.

Puddephat, Wilfrid. "The Mural Paintings of the Dance of Death in the Guild Chapel of Stratford-upon-Avon." *Birmingham Archaeological Society Transactions* 76 (1960): 29–35.

Rastall, Richard. "Music and Liturgy in *Everyman*: Some Aspects of Production." *Leeds Studies in English*, n.s. 29 (1998): 305–14.

Riehle, Wolfgang. *The Middle English Mystics*. Trans. Bernard Standring. London: Routledge and Kegan Paul, 1981.

Rogers, Nicholas. "The Particular Judgement: Two Earlier Examples of a Motif in Jan Mostaert's Lost Self-Portrait." *Oud Holland* (1983): 125–27.

The Rohan Master: A Book of Hours: Bibliothèque Nationale, Paris, MS. Latin 9471. New York: Braziller, 1973.

Roper, William. *The Lyfe of Sir Thomas Moore, Knighte*. Ed. Elsie Vaughan Hitchcock. EETS o.s. 197. London: Oxford University Press, 1935.

Ryan, Lawrence V. "Doctrine and Dramatic Structure in *Everyman*." *Speculum* 32 (1957): 722–35.

Salter, K. W. "*Lear* and the Morality Tradition." *Notes and Queries* 199 (1954): 110.

Schmitt, Natalie Crohn. "The Idea of a Person in Medieval Morality Plays." *Comparative Drama* 12 (1978): 23–34.

Schreiber, Earl G. "*Everyman* in America." *Comparative Drama* 9 (1975): 99–115.

Shakespeare, William. *The Riverside Shakespeare*. Ed. G. Blakemore Evans et al. Boston: Houghton-Mifflin, 1997.

Sir Thomas More. In *The Shakespeare Apocrypha, Being a Collection of Fourteen Plays Which Have Been Ascribed to Shakespeare*. Ed. C. F. Tucker Brooke. Oxford: Clarendon Press, 1918.

Slack, Paul. "Mortality Crises and Epidemic Disease in England 1485–1610." In *Health, Medicine and Mortality in the Sixteenth Century*. Ed. Charles Webster. Cambridge: Cambridge University Press, 1979. Pp. 9–59.

Speaight, Robert. *William Poel and the Elizabethan Revival*. London: William Heinemann, 1954.

Spinrad, Phoebe S. "The Last Temptation of Everyman." *Philological Quarterly* 64 (1985): 185–94.

———. *The Summons of Death on the Medieval and Renaissance English Stage*. Columbus: Ohio State University Press, 1987.

Tasker, Edward G. *Encyclopedia of Medieval Church Art*. London: B. T. Batsford, 1993.

Tigg, E. R. "Is *Elckerlijc* prior to *Everyman*?" *Journal of English and Germanic Philology* 38 (1939): 568–96.

———. "Is *Elckerlijc* prior to *Everyman*?" *Neophilologus* 26 (1941): 121–41.

Tilley, Morris Palmer. *Elizabethan Proverb Lore*. New York: Macmillan, 1926.

———. *A Dictionary of the Proverbs in England in the Sixteenth and Seventeenth Centuries*. Ann Arbor: University of Michigan Press, 1950.

The Towneley Plays. Ed. Martin Stevens and A. C. Cawley. 2 vols. EETS s.s. 13–14. Oxford: Oxford University Press, 1994.

Tristram, Philippa. *Figures of Life and Death in Medieval English Literature*. New York: New York University Press, 1976.

Turner, Victor. "Liminal to Liminoid in Play, Flow, and Ritual: An Essay in Comparative Symbiology." *Rice University Studies* 60 (1974): 53–92.

Van Laan, Thomas F. "*Everyman:* A Structural Analysis." *PMLA* 78 (1963): 465–75.

Vocht, Henry de. *Everyman: A Comparative Study of Texts and Sources*. Louvain: Uystpruyst, 1947.

Vos, R. "De datering van de Elckerlijc." *Spiegel der Letteren* 9 (1965–66): 101–09.

Walker, Greg. *The Politics of Performance in Early Renaissance Drama*. Cambridge: Cambridge University Press, 1998.

Wasson, John. "The Morality Play: Ancestor of Elizabethan Drama?" *Comparative Drama* 13 (1979): 210–21.

Whiting, Bartlett Jere, and Helen Wescott Whiting. *Proverbs, Sentences and Proverbial Phrases from English Writings, Mainly before 1500*. Cambridge, MA: Harvard University Press, 1968.

Wilson, Edward. *A Descriptive Index of the English Lyrics in John of Grimestone's Preaching Book*. Medium Ævum Monographs, n.s. 2. Oxford: Blackwell, for the Society for the Study of Mediaeval Languages and Literature, 1973.

Wood, Francis A. "*Elckerlijc–Everyman*: The Question of Priority." *Modern Philology* 8 (1910): 279–302.

Woolf, Rosemary. *The English Religious Lyric in the Middle Ages*. Oxford: Clarendon Press, 1968.

The Worlde and the Childe. Ed. Clifford Davidson and Peter Happé. Kalamazoo, MI: Medieval Institute Publications, 1999.

MIDDLE ENGLISH TEXTS SERIES

The Floure and the Leafe, The Assembly of Ladies, The Isle of Ladies, edited by Derek Pearsall (1990)
Three Middle English Charlemagne Romances, edited by Alan Lupack (1990)
Six Ecclesiastical Satires, edited by James M. Dean (1991)
Heroic Women from the Old Testament in Middle English Verse, edited by Russell A. Peck (1991)
The Canterbury Tales: Fifteenth-Century Continuations and Additions, edited by John M. Bowers (1992)
Gavin Douglas, *The Palis of Honoure*, edited by David Parkinson (1992)
Wynnere and Wastoure and The Parlement of the Thre Ages, edited by Warren Ginsberg (1992)
The Shewings of Julian of Norwich, edited by Georgia Ronan Crampton (1994)
King Arthur's Death: The Middle English Stanzaic Morte Arthur and Alliterative Morte Arthure, edited by Larry D. Benson, revised by Edward E. Foster (1994)
Lancelot of the Laik and Sir Tristrem, edited by Alan Lupack (1994)
Sir Gawain: Eleven Romances and Tales, edited by Thomas Hahn (1995)
The Middle English Breton Lays, edited by Anne Laskaya and Eve Salisbury (1995)
Sir Perceval of Galles and Ywain and Gawain, edited by Mary Flowers Braswell (1995)
Four Middle English Romances: Sir Isumbras, Octavian, Sir Eglamour of Artois, Sir Tryamour, edited by Harriet Hudson (1996; second edition 2006)
The Poems of Laurence Minot 1333–1352, edited by Richard H. Osberg (1996)
Medieval English Political Writings, edited by James M. Dean (1996)
The Book of Margery Kempe, edited by Lynn Staley (1996)
Amis and Amiloun, Robert of Cisyle, and Sir Amadace, edited by Edward E. Foster (1997)
The Cloud of Unknowing, edited by Patrick J. Gallacher (1997)
Robin Hood and Other Outlaw Tales, edited by Stephen Knight and Thomas Ohlgren (1997; second edition 2000)
The Poems of Robert Henryson, edited by Robert L. Kindrick with assistance of Kristie A. Bixby (1997)
Moral Love Songs and Laments, edited by Susanna Greer Fein (1998)
John Lydgate, *Troy Book Selections*, edited by Robert R. Edwards (1998)
Thomas Usk, *The Testament of Love*, edited by R. Allen Shoaf (1998)
Prose Merlin, edited by John Conlee (1998)
Middle English Marian Lyrics, edited by Karen Saupe (1998)
John Metham, *Amoryus and Cleopes*, edited by Stephen F. Page (1999)
Four Romances of England: King Horn, Havelok the Dane, Bevis of Hampton, Athelston, edited by Ronald B. Herzman, Graham Drake, and Eve Salisbury (1999)
The Assembly of Gods: Le Assemble de Dyeus, or Banquet of Gods and Goddesses, with the Discourse of Reason and Sensuality, edited by Jane Chance (1999)
Thomas Hoccleve, *The Regiment of Princes*, edited by Charles R. Blyth (1999)
John Capgrave, *The Life of Saint Katherine*, edited by Karen A. Winstead (1999)
John Gower, *Confessio Amantis*, Vol. 1, edited by Russell A. Peck; with Latin translations by Andrew Galloway (2000; second edition 2006); Vol. 2 (2003); Vol. 3 (2004)
Richard the Redeless and Mum and the Sothsegger, edited by James M. Dean (2000)
Ancrene Wisse, edited by Robert Hasenfratz (2000)
Walter Hilton, *The Scale of Perfection*, edited by Thomas H. Bestul (2000)
John Lydgate, *The Siege of Thebes*, edited by Robert R. Edwards (2001)
Pearl, edited by Sarah Stanbury (2001)
The Trials and Joys of Marriage, edited by Eve Salisbury (2002)

Middle English Legends of Women Saints, edited by Sherry L. Reames, with assistance of
    Martha G. Blalock and Wendy R. Larson (2003)
The Wallace: Selections, edited by Anne McKim (2003)
Richard Maidstone, *Concordia (The Reconciliation of Richard II with London)*, edited by
    David R. Carlson, with a verse translation by A. G. Rigg (2003)
Three Purgatory Poems: The Gast of Gy, Sir Owain, The Vision of Tundale, edited by Edward
    E. Foster (2004)
William Dunbar, *The Complete Works*, edited by John Conlee (2004)
Chaucerian Dream Visions and Complaints, edited by Dana M. Symons (2004)
Stanzaic Guy of Warwick, edited by Alison Wiggins (2004)
Saints' Lives in Middle English Collections, edited by E. Gordon Whatley, with Anne B.
    Thompson and Robert K. Upchurch (2004)
Siege of Jerusalem, edited by Michael Livingston (2004)
The Kingis Quair and Other Prison Poems, edited by Linne R. Mooney and Mary-Jo Arn
    (2005)
Chaucerian Apocrypha: Selections, edited by Kathleen Forni (2005)
John Gower, *The Minor Latin Works*, edited and translated by R. F. Yeager, with *In Praise
    of Peace*, edited by Michael Livingston (2005)
*Sentimental and Humorous Romances: Floris and Blancheflour, Sir Degrevant, The Squire of
    Low Degree, The Tournament of Tottenham, and The Feast of Tottenham*, edited by Erik
    Kooper (2006)
Dicts and Sayings of the Philosophers, edited by John William Sutton (2006)

DOCUMENTS OF PRACTICE SERIES

Love and Marriage in Late Medieval London, selected, translated, and introduced by
    Shannon McSheffrey (1995)
Sources for the History of Medicine in Late Medieval England, selected, introduced, and
    translated by Carole Rawcliffe (1995)
A Slice of Life: Selected Documents of Medieval English Peasant Experience, edited, translated,
    and with an introduction by Edwin Brezette DeWindt (1996)
Regular Life: Monastic, Canonical, and Mendicant Rules, selected and introduced by
    Douglas J. McMillan and Kathryn Smith Fladenmuller (1997); second edition,
    selected and introduced by Daniel Marcel La Corte and Douglas J. McMillan (2004)
Women and Monasticism in Medieval Europe: Sisters and Patrons of the Cistercian Reform,
    selected, translated, and with an introduction by Constance H. Berman (2002)
Medieval Notaries and Their Acts: The 1327–1328 Register of Jean Holanie, introduced,
    edited, and translated by Kathryn L. Reyerson and Debra A. Salata (2004)

COMMENTARY SERIES

Haimo of Auxerre, *Commentary on the Book of Jonah*, translated with an introduction and
    notes by Deborah Everhart (1993)
Medieval Exegesis in Translation: Commentaries on the Book of Ruth, translated with an intro-
    duction and notes by Lesley Smith (1996)
Nicholas of Lyra's Apocalypse Commentary, translated with an introduction and notes by
    Philip D. W. Krey (1997)

Rabbi Ezra Ben Solomon of Gerona, *Commentary on the Song of Songs and Other Kabbalistic Commentaries*, selected, translated, and annotated by Seth Brody (1999)

John Wyclif, *On the Truth of Holy Scripture*, translated with an introduction and notes by Ian Christopher Levy (2001)

Second Thessalonians: Two Early Medieval Apocalyptic Commentaries, introduced and translated by Steven R. Cartwright and Kevin L. Hughes (2001)

The Glossa Ordinaria on the Song of Songs, translated with an introduction and notes by Mary Dove (2004)

MEDIEVAL GERMAN TEXTS IN BILINGUAL EDITIONS SERIES

Sovereignty and Salvation in the Vernacular, 1050–1150, introduction, translations, and notes by James A. Schultz (2000)

Ava's New Testament Narratives: "When the Old Law Passed Away," introduction, translation, and notes by James A. Rushing, Jr. (2003)

History as Literature: German World Chronicles of the Thirteenth Century in Verse, introduction, translation, and notes by R. Graeme Dunphy (2003)

VARIA

The Study of Chivalry: Resources and Approaches, edited by Howell Chickering and Thomas H. Seiler (1988)

Studies in the Harley Manuscript: The Scribes, Contents, and Social Contexts of British Library MS Harley 2253, edited by Susanna Fein (2000)

The Liturgy of the Medieval Church, edited by Thomas J. Heffernan and E. Ann Matter (2001); second edition (2005)

TO ORDER PLEASE CONTACT:

Medieval Institute Publications
Western Michigan University
Kalamazoo, MI 49008-5432
Phone (269) 387-8755
FAX (269) 387-8750

http://www.wmich.edu/medieval/mip/index.html

Medieval Institute Publications is a program
of The Medieval Institute, College of Arts
and Sciences, Western Michigan University

Typeset in 10/13 New Baskerville
with Golden Cockerel Ornaments display
Designed by Linda K. Judy
Manufactured by McNaughton-Gunn, Inc.

Medieval Institute Publications
College of Arts and Sciences
Western Michigan University
1903 W. Michigan Avenue
Kalamazoo, MI 49008-5432
http://www.wmich.edu/medieval/mip

 WESTERN MICHIGAN UNIVERSITY